Milo

by

Daphne Mills

DORRANCE PUBLISHING CO
EST. 1920
PITTSBURGH, PENNSYLVANIA 15238

Dorrance Publishing Co
585 Alpha Drive
Pittsburgh, PA 15238
Visit our website at www.dorrancebookstore.com

ISBN: 979-8-8860-4368-6
eISBN: 979-8-8860-4461-4

CHAPTER ONE

"Have you prepared the way of the Lord? Have you made your paths straight?" Bishop Gavin Parker said to the congregation. Tall with a mustache standing behind the podium, in a ten by twenty square foot capacity of about 300. His thunderous voice filled the sanctuary. His suit, purple pants, jacket, and vest. The handkerchief in his left breast pocket and tie blue with a black shirt.

"Welcome to New Walk baptist Church. We are glad to see you supporting the youth department, thanks for coming. If anyone needs a program, let the ushers know and they will give you one. I am going to get out of the way; the next voice you will hear is from Mrs. Queen McQueen, the youth director."

Mrs. Queen's dress was purple, white, and black with purple shoes. Slender, short in stature, she walked up and took the microphone. "Thank you, Bishop," she turned and faced the congregation. "I would like to thank all of you for coming out this evening to be with our youth. They have worked so hard putting everything together. To start they will sing a song, a skit will be performed, praise and mime dancers, and much more. You have your programs to follow along. Now we will turn it over to the youth choir."

The congregation applauded as the choir director came to the platform. The director, Mrs. Nina Frost, sturdy stocky body, charcoal gray hair, overbite. White robe with a purple V-neck raised her right hand as the musician dressed in all black began to play. The choir in purple robes started to sing Jesus loves me while the mime and praise dancers matching began to perform. The music saturated the sanctuary, booming out of the large speakers on the platform. Every movement also could be seen on the big screen behind the choir stand.

Seven-year-old Milo Ice, round coffee-brown eyes, thin eyebrows, dark skin smooth with sharp cheekbones. Sitting in the pews with his mother, Martha Ice, swinging his legs because of not wanting to be there. He had other plans, but his mother wanted him in church. As the music and singing filled the church, Milo became mesmerized by the combination. He stopped swinging his legs and leaned onto the pew in front of him. No one was in front of him, he could see the performance very well. The music penetrated the young man's soul and his heartbeat to the rhythm of the notes, with the words talking just to him. When everything was over, he sought out the minister of music, Cole Brady.

He was short, stout, with a snub nose and a gap in his teeth. Looking over his glasses while gathering up the sheet music.

Milo approached him and said, "Excuse me, sir, I am acquiring to join the musicians."

Cole insisted, "What can you do?"

Milo indicated, "Don't know, but I can learn." Cole stepped back, putting his rough hands on his mouth. Looking at Milo, not believing what he just said to him.

He said to Milo, "You are wasting my minutes. I do not have time to teach you, neither do my musicians. We run this place; we are the stars of the show. You will not make me look bad not knowing anything. This is all about perfection; did you hear me? I will repeat it again just in case you didn't. I said this is all about perfection, now leave me alone. I have work to do." Milo kept going; he went to the choir director. Mrs. Nina was talking to one of the choir members when he came to ask about joining.

Milo said to her, "Excuse me, Mrs. Nina, I would like to join the singers."

Mrs. Nina blurted out, "What octave do you use?"

Milo mumbled, "I do not know what octave means."

Mrs. Nina stated, "First of all, you will have to sing out loud. If you are mumbling now, you will not be able to sing for this group. Also, if you do not know what octave means, then you will mess up this harmonization. In this assembly, you must be able to carry a tune. By the looks of you, that is not going to happen. We know that your mother cannot sing, only good for running a copy machine."

Milo was about to let her have it talking about his mother like that, but he decided against it. He wanted to be a part of this if she would let him. He tried one more time to convince her.

"Mrs. Nina, I can learn if you just let me in, ma'am."

Mrs. Nina, frustrated, spoke, "As I told you before, you must be able to carry a tune; the answer is still no, now leave me, boy." Milo's next travel was to the mime leader Trey Bond. Trey, white with a black shirt, pants with white gloves. Suspenders turned backwards, face puffed as if a bee had stung him. Milo felt confident that he would get this one by being a great dancer. He approached Trey in one of the classrooms and asked him if he could join the mimes. Trey wanted to know if he knew anything about being a mime. Milo shook his head, then cut a move. He explained to Milo that this was more than just dancing. Mime is an art form of speaking, through music and dance, facial features and gestures.

They who do this must be well-trained in storytelling. They must know how to entertain without using words. Silence is the key; they must deliver the message by expressing themselves through these essentials. Discipline, which is important to this art, it educates and helps the person stay focused. They must be able to connect with the audience, making the onlookers feel with their eyes what they are bringing. If one can achieve this, success is unavoidable.

"Milo, the mime team works with the music section, you must be accepted by Cole," mentioned Trey.

Milo thanked him for what he had taught him in such a short period of time. Cole already told him no, he must be on with his search. Leaving the classroom, Milo went looking for Grace Walker, the praise dancer. A ballerina who walks as her name with grace. Grace is a tall, slim woman who walks with her head held high. Palms facing downward as she walks. When he saw her, she was heading towards the pastor's office. Moving towards her, he called out her name; she turned around as if she was dancing. He asked her if he could become a member of the praise team.

Grace said to Milo, "What do you know about being a praise dancer? Or better yet, can you even dance?"

He said, "Yes, I can dance, but I do not know about being a praise dancer. Can you be able to help me become one?"

Grace explained, "Praise dancing is the whirl of fabric and motion. With arms lifted up and the storytelling communicates emotions of gratitude. Praise is an alternative to words; your experiences of God testifies. You must be called to dance.

The body and spirit must be united. You must dance like Miriam, sister of Moses, who took a tambourine and led the women into a dance after the parting of the red sea. This was an expression of joy and celebration after God's great miracle on their behalf." Grace explained that Cole was the leader of the praise team. He is responsible for the recruiting, assigning, and training. Milo was stunned to know that he trains. He wondered why he didn't take the time to train him?

Milo told Grace that he already said no to him; he thanked Grace and walked off. One more person to talk to before he decides to call it quits. He went to look for the youth leader. He walked out of the church, and Mrs. Queen was going to her car, a Bugatti Veyron Sport white with red seats, when Milo called out to her. Catching up to her, she turned around to see who was calling her. When he approached, asked if she would be so kind as to let him in the youth group.

Mrs. Queen questioned him, "Why do you want to be in the youth group, son?"

Stunned by what she asked, he continued, "First I would like to know if Cole is the head of this."

She said, "No, he is not."

He said, "Okay then, how can I become a part of the group?"

Mrs. Queen smiled and said, "Just by asking. Milo, welcome to the youth group." Milo jumped up and down, finally he became part of a group in New Walk Baptist Church. He thanked Mrs. Queen, turning away, ran to find his mother. Martha Ice and Pastor Gavin were standing on the porch of the church. He walked up and stood at the bottom of the stairs, waiting for them to finish talking to tell his mother the good news. When they noticed him, they ended their conversation, and the pastor walked in the church. Martha walked down the stairs and greeted her son with a kiss.

CHAPTER TWO

His mother said, "Milo, I saw you and Queen talking, what did she want with you?"

Her son responded, "She did not want anything, I was the one wanting. I spent all this time trying to get into one of the ministries. Everyone pointed me back to the first person who rudely told me no. She was the only one that said yes. Every group had a separate name, but it was run by one person. Cole Brady. The youth leader knows how to treat someone who wants to be a part of them. She showed me how someone new can be welcomed in New Walk Baptist church."

Martha Ice smiled at Milo and held on to the statement of knowing how to make a newcomer feel welcome in the church.

**

The day of the first meeting for Milo to start the youth group had come. He hollered for his mother, who was still getting dressed, "Mom, will you hurry up? I am going to be late." He walked in the kitchen to fix himself a glass of water. He turned around to holler again for his mother. Martha was standing at the door; she let him know that for someone who does not want to be late, he is really taking his time to get out of the door. Milo and Martha left the house and headed to the church. Merging onto I-74 toward Winston-Salem, she merges onto I-40 toward Winston-Salem and Mount Airy onto US-52 to Akron Drive. Turn left onto Indiana Avenue, slightly left onto North Cherry Street. Turn right and proceed down the hill to the church.

Martha parked the car at the youth center and walked Milo in the building. He walked up to the receptionist, who gave him a clipboard to find his name, then pointed him in the direction of the classroom they were meeting in. Martha gave him a hug and left the building. Milo went into the computer room. As he entered, Mrs. Queen was sitting at her desk typing on the computer. She smiled at him and told him to choose a seat. He went to the desk next to a girl , who introduced herself as Jade Summers. She pointed to a young boy on her left side and introduced him as her brother, Nico Summers.

Nico was very quiet, he just looked up and smiled. Mrs. Queen rose up out of her chair and introduced Milo to the rest of the group. She explained to Milo what the group consisted of.

"In this group, I encourage all youths to learn more about faith and become more involved in their spiritual life. We provide the common good in viewpoint, finances, and political discipline, also wealth, general welfare, and public benefits. The common good is beneficial to all of a given community in the realm of government and public services. Summer camps are a part of this group, organizing events and activities, including religious instructions and pastoral oversight.

I encourage practices of coming to Sunday school. The group starts late afternoon, before attending an evening service of worship Wednesday and Friday nights. Some Saturdays are required also. I will make an announcement when the time comes. We are student led where the students take on responsibilities of planning services. Now, Milo, are you willing to take on all these tasks?"

"Yes, I will with great loyalty, ma'am, " he said.

The ages of the youth were from seven to eighteen. They developed physically, socially, mentally, and emotionally. They received experience of leadership by organizing programs for the different activities in science, political, biblical, and socializing. The group participates in yoga, dance, learning to play different instruments, mime, and singing. All the things Milo did not know how to do, he will learn how to do. He will be able from this moment to get into any other group he wants to. Jade helped him, she was very knowledgeable, and everyone looked to her for what they had problems with. Jade had many skills in being a leader. She worked very hard at becoming a leader to take over the youth group one day. Everyone knew that she would be the chosen one. As the time went on, Mrs. Queen took a liking to Milo; she called on him for special tasks. She was pleased with him.

"He is the one," laughed Mrs. Queen.

Jade became disturbed by the friendliness of the youth leader and Milo. The young lady was not going to let this newcomer take what rightfully belongs to her. She will find a way to make him less desirable in her eyes. The girl got with her brother to come up with ideas to make Milo less loyal to Mrs. Queen. Jade and Nico went off by themselves when it was time to go outside. Sitting on the tables at the far side of the fenced yard, with pencil and paper, they jotted down what they would do to discredit Milo.

Mrs. Queen saw Jade and Nico at the table by themselves and walked over to them. They were busy trying to write down the disgrace of Milo that they did not see her walk up. She grabbed the paper from the both of them. Not looking at the paper, she let them know of the rule of being by themselves and not mingling with others. She pointed for them to get back with the group. Nico and Jade walked back over to the group and started on the activity of the day. Jade wondered if Mrs. Queen would read the paper that they had written on. Mrs. Queen put the paper in her skirt pocket and walked over to the group.

"We have thirty more minutes before it is time for everyone to go home. Your parents will be out front waiting for you, so go and get ready to go home," Mrs. Queen instructed. The youth all ran in the building to get ready to go home. Jade and Nico walking slowly, paused when they got near Mrs. Queen holding open the door.

She smiled and said to them, "See you next week." Jade and Nico smiled and went to pack their stuff to exit the building. The parents were lined up as always, each child came out one by one to get in the cars. Waving good-bye to Mrs. Queen, they left, and she went back into the building. Grabbing the papers out of her skirt, she saw the plot that Jade and Nico were planning for Milo. At the next meeting, Milo was to lead the biblical program for the pastor. They were planning to sabotage his speech. Milo did not know too much about the scriptures in the bible. Jade always helped him understand what he was reading.

She promised to write out his speech to impress the pastor on his becoming a member of the youth group. Instead of writing about a character of the bible, he was going to be reading about a character in a horror movie. They were going to change the name of the bible characters as characters of a movie.

Milo would not know the difference because he did not know enough about the bible like Jade and Nico. Mrs. Queen pondered why Jade and Nico would do something like this. It did not make any sense seeing that Jade loved to help everybody in the group. Nico of course only followed after Jade. The lady looked at every twist and turn since Milo came to the group.

A light bulb went off. She used to call on Jade, who loved to help everybody, and now she is calling on Milo. Mrs. Queen now understands why the disgrace and shame has come into the mist of the group. She was so glad that she came across the paper before Milo stood up in front of the congregation and the pastor. Jade was a leader, but she was not loyal. She wanted to be the next youth leader, but she did not have all of the qualifications as Milo has. He has a calling on his life and he is following his heart. If your heart's not in it, it will not last. You must have mercy, compassion, and goodwill towards others. Milo has all those qualities while Jade just knows how to get things organized.

"I will have to write up a paper for him, just in case Jade and Nico want to follow their plan of treachery," she said. Mrs. Queen jumped up and down smiling that she stopped the principalities right in their tracks.

CHAPTER THREE

Mrs. Queen started straightening up the meeting room. She gathered the books to put them back on the shelf. She looked around the room to see if anything else needed to be put away or thrown away. Not seeing anything, she headed to her desk and proceeded to finish the logbook attendance for the youth. Not too many kids came today; she only had to record ten out of the usual twenty-five. This put a smile on her face knowing she would get home early. When she finished the last entry, she looked one last time to make sure of not missing anything. She walked across the room and turned off the lights and shut the door.

She was overjoyed about presenting to the pastor her request about Milo. It was all set up for him to take the position of youth leader when he comes of age. Mrs. Queen saw that she was the last to go home. She left the letter for the pastor just in case she could not speak for herself, the letter would speak for her. She would be an elder when he reaches the age to take over the center. Planning for everything is her motto. On her exit from the church, she set the alarm and locked the door behind her. It was a hot night as she walked towards her car. She heard a noise behind her, looking back as she walked but not seeing anyone. Mrs. Queen hurried to the car just in case someone was there. Coming up to the Bugatti Veyron Sport, the woman reached in her pocketbook to retrieve her keys. Attempting to unlock the car door, a man came up behind and grabbed her around the neck.

The man whispered in her ear to get undressed. Pressure being applied to her throat, all that was left on was her shoes. He was already undressed, intoxicated; he had a yearning for her body, bending her over, he started to rape her. She did not say anything as he forced her to perform disgusting acts on him; he beat and raped her repeatedly. When the act was finished, he asked if there was some gratification. She said yes, hoping it would help let her go. The assailant told her not to tell anyone of what had happened. If she didn't, she would not have to ever worry about him again. Mrs. Queen at this time felt filthy; any morality that she had was no longer left in her. The lady believed she was no longer a decent valued Christian woman, now just fleshly. Mrs. Queen questioned the man.

"Why do you want to take advantage of a poor, helpless old woman? You could have gotten any young person that could give you more pleasure."

The young man said, "You should be glad to finally have a good time. I only came for one thing but got a bonus in the process." He asked her to give him the keys to the car. The old lady was not tolerating any more oppression. No matter what happens, she was not yielding to this man, the car which her late husband gave. She was willing and ready to die rather than to agree. All fear left, and bravery took its place to stand up against the boy. All guilt and shame was gone from being brutally assaulted. He did not treat her as a woman, he treated her mercilessly, no respect. He did not see her as she should be seen. Treated her less than a human; he was brutal.

Angrily she said, "You felt that you had the right to my body, but you will not have the right to my car. While I still have breath in my body, there is nothing you do that will get me to agree to part with it." He slapped her, and she slapped him back, and they began to tussle.

The young man smiled and said, "You have more strength than a young woman, I love a woman with fire." He put pressure on her, but she defended herself with all that she had. Mrs. Queen, worn and tired from all her struggles, started running away from the young man, but he was too quick. He grabbed her again around the neck and cut her throat. She slid down beside the car, putting both hands around her throat. When the young man saw the limpness of the woman, he felt remorse, but the fear of going back to jail made him drag her away from the door, removed the keys from the woman's tight clenched hand, then took the car. He left her dying with her shoes on in the parking lot of the church.

***

Bishop Gavin, sitting in his study room, started to feel a chill over his body. He wondered how he could be so cold when it was so hot. He grabbed a sweater anyway and continued to study. He began to read, He was oppressed and He was afflicted, yet he opened not his mouth; He was brought as a lamb to the slaughter. Gavin paused, and the chill was as if it was to his bones, he went to get a throw cover. The pastor started looking in his briefcase to find his appointment book; it was not there. He looked all over the house, he must have left it at the church. He left his house to return to the church to pick up the book.

***

As the clergy turned on the street where New Walk Baptist was located, he parked in front of the steps of the church and went in to retrieve the appointment book. On exiting the church, he saw something move in the parking lot. He set the alarm and locked the door of the church. He went to see what was in the parking lot; when he came near, he noticed that it was Mrs. Queen. All battered and bleeding, he knelt down beside her and he put his arms around her and covered her naked body with the throw cover. At the moment he put the cover over her, life left her. He now understood why he had the chills and grabbed the throw rug. The scripture spoke of oppression, affliction, and slaughter. The condition of Mrs. Queen's body went through all three.

Pastor Gavin knew he had to pull himself together and call the police. Upon the police arrival, he told all that he knew, which was nothing but finding the body all battered and bruised.

The police questioned the pastor, "Did you see or hear anyone? Did you touch the body?"

The minister said, "I did not see or hear anyone, but I did touch the body, putting her in my arms and covering her with that throw before she expired."

While the police document the pastor's statement, the detectives arrive on the scene. The CSI unit just finished assessing, documenting, and canvassing the area. The detective walked over to the officer and asked them what they gathered.

The officer explained, "When we arrived, the pastor was the only one on the scene, he's right over there by the tree."

The detective said, "Thank you, officer, we will take it from here." They began to investigate the area where the body was found, determining physical evidence and defining the dimensions of the crime scene. They placed the evidence tagged in a bag properly marked for identification later. After accessing the scene, the body was released to be sent to the autopsy. They prepared and executed a search warrant for the church since it was private property. The detectives approached the pastor, introduced themselves as Louis Walsh, large ears, uncut hair, full pursed lips, blue eyes, and dressed in a wrinkled black suit. Detective Chance Finn, clean cut with precise features, brown eyes, dressed in a cleaner pressed suit. Investigator Finn asked the pastor what kind of car did the deceased drive?

Pastor Gavin responded, "She drove a Bugatti Veyron Sport."

Detective Finn said, "This could be tied to the thieves who take expensive sports cars to chop shops. We will be back with a warrant to search the church and the youth center." The detectives left the grounds. Pastor Gavin was left alone, he looked around and saw the crime scene, picturing the battered and bruised body of Mrs. Queen. As she was lying dying in his arms, he was glad that he was there with her, so she would not have to die alone. Walking toward the church, he felt his legs weaken; he had to embrace himself. He paused for a moment, then went to his office to call the mothers.

He picked up the phone and saw that it was eleven o'clock, too late to call now. He put back down the receiver. Locking up the church, he left and went home. For some reason the drive home from the church seemed much longer than it used to take.

CHAPTER FOUR

The next morning, Pastor Gavin, arriving earlier than usual to the church, called the mothers of the youth group. He told them of the passing of the youth leader and he would give them further notice about when the children can come back to the youth center. As he was hanging up the phone, Martha Ice entered his office. He did not greet her as usual, he was not himself. She asked what was wrong. Standing up he motioned for her to sit down.

Martha asked, "What is the matter with you this morning, pastor?"

Gavin stated, "Sit down, Martha, I have to tell you something. I waited for you to come in this morning to tell you the news."

Martha added, "What news would that be about, pastor Gavin?"

He mouthed, "Last night, when I had to come back to New Walk, I found Mrs. Queen dying in the parking lot. She died in my arms. On top of that, she left me a letter wanting Milo to be the next youth leader if she is not around. Imagine that."

Martha gasped, "Oh, pastor, who would want to do that to a sweet woman like her?"

Gavin expressed, "I don't know, I waited for you to come in so you could prepare yourself to tell Milo. You know how much he really cared for her."

Martha threw out, "Yes, I know how fond they were of each other. You will have to pass on the news about the youth leader position yourself, she placed it in your hands."

Gavin piped, "I have to take a moment, Martha, this is heavy on me right at this moment. Will you please excuse me?"

"I will not let anyone disturb you till you are ready," promised Martha.

"Thank you, Martha, appreciate you," mouthed Gavin.

Martha left the office, put up a do not disturb sign, then started her daily routine. As she did her duties, she wondered about what she would say to Milo. How would he react? Is he able to understand death? What would she do if he does not take it well? The phone rang to snap her out of her pondering. The person on the other end was a woman grief counselor that Mrs. Queen had set up a training class for the youth to learn about grief. What a coincidence, this is what she needed. She could get her questions answered. Martha let it be known that the lady passed, but she set up the appointment for her to still come.

***

Milo felt like crying, and he did not have any reason to cry. Sitting on the bench in front of the children's mental health, waiting to do his community service for the youth group. He shook the feeling away as he waited for the instructor to come and sign him in. Tears began to flow. When Milo wiped his eyes, he saw an angel standing on his right side. Milo jumped at the appearance of the messenger; he was troubled, and fear fell upon him.

The angel pronounced, "Fear not, Milo, for I have heard your heart's cry. You shall receive strength and joy, many shall rejoice with you. Great are you in the eyes of the Lord. It was good that you personally chose the children's mental health. Milo, you will turn many children to the Lord, our God. Turning the hearts of the children from disobedience to obedience. Making the children ready and preparing the way for the Lord."

Milo said, "How shall I do this, seeing that I am only seven-years-old?"

The divine being continued, "You will receive what you need when the time comes. Nothing is impossible with God."

Milo responded, "Okay, if you say this is so, let it be as you have told me. By the way, what is your name?"

"I am Gabriel, an archangel, your messenger. Milo, you are about to face something, that is why you cried. I need you to guard your heart, blessed is he who believes. There will be a manifestation of the things which were told to you from the Lord." Milo looked down and wondered what he meant by guarding his heart, and what was he going to face? He could not believe that he was chosen for a task such as this. Milo turned to ask the angel why he was chosen, but the angel was gone. The instructor walked up, they went into the children's mental health. Milo saw through different lenses; his perspective had changed since the heavenly visitation.

Milo worked with the three to seven-year-olds. The children have significant social, emotional, and behavioral challenges that cause disruption in the home and school. The children are definite, lose their temper, and refuse to apply to rules set by adults. The young boy took a deep breath; with what the angel spoke and what he was about to face with these kids, he put his best face forward. Walking in the bare room, nothing but soft mats. He went over to the three boys. Malik, hands over his eyes looking like a blotched fighter. Malik and dirt just go together like sweet and sour. Ronin, small head with a large cap, and his clothes falling off his narrow shoulders, everything too big for his thin body. Zeke did not look like much of anything important at all. His smile was easy to understand but scarce.

Milo looked at the boys and smiled with the understanding that he would turn the hearts of the children from disobedience to obedience. If all the children he encounters are like these boys, he will have his work cut out for him. Malik, who was the leader of the group, saw Milo. The boys ran up and welcomed him, then went in their usual corner and all sat on the mats. The instructor walked up to the area, and all three boys went into resentment of the instructor disrespecting their area. Talking hateful and mean to the adult to get away from their territory. The three boys teamed up, pushing and shoving the counselor. First time dealing with the boys, the instructor didn't know how to handle them. Tackling the teacher down on the floor, they began to fight, being cruel to the woman. Milo stepped in and asked the boys to let go of the instructor. Yelling that she was an adult and was not allowed in their corner. Milo explained that she was a substitute and did not know the rules. If they would let her go, he would make sure she would not come back over disrespecting the corner. They liked Milo, he was a kid himself and understood territory.

They agreed and let the adult go, who ran out of the room. Milo finished up his day, no adult came near the corner. They gave Milo props for helping keep them away. Smiling to himself, boy, maybe I do have a gift of turning the hearts of the children. Walking out of mental health, his mother was outside waiting. He waved to the instructor and got in the car with his mother. Milo started to tell his mother about the incident with the boys and the instructor of the youth group. The mention of the youth group, she paused before she drove off. Staring out the front window with both hands on the steering wheel, Martha did not know how to start to tell him.

Milo broke the silence, "Mom, why did you come to pick me up?" Martha, still looking out of the window, remained silent. Milo gave her a shove on her shoulder to shake her out of her state. She still remained silent. He called her name, and she still remained silent. Milo began to fear not knowing if she was sick or not; he began to panic. Milo opened the car door to go back into mental health to get someone to help her. They suggest he call an ambulance; they only help mental children. Letting them know that she was having a mental issue qualifies. He was getting nowhere with this receptionist. He went back outside and got back in the car. Milo tried again to get his mother's attention; she turned to him and smiled at him, took a deep breath, and blew it out slowly. Milo looked on, at least she is responding this time. Martha put her hand on his shoulder and let him know that Mrs. Queen had died. He turned and put both hands on the dash and stared out the window.

CHAPTER FIVE

Milo is stunned he has lost his mentor. As he sat at Southwest Middle School, staring out the window, many thoughts rushed in his head. Milo decided that he needed to get up and leave this place to go find the killer. His teacher Mr. Zayn Stucky, with long and greasy hair, biddy eyes, long beard plated with a ring on the end. Tall in stature, well-dressed. Mr. Stucky called out to him to pay attention to what was going on in the class, not staring out the window. This was Milo's chance to walk out; he got up, looked at the teacher, and mentioned that there were more interesting things outside that window than what he was teaching in the class.

Milo walked out of the class and left the school. Not knowing where he was going, but he knew he had to keep walking. Milo came upon this chop shop, a young boy looking about thirteen was leaning up against a scrap can. Milo looked inside the shop and saw all of the beautiful cars. He asked what they do in the shop. The young man responded about the cars being stolen, and they dismantled them to sell the parts.

"Would you like to see how?"

"Yes, that's amazing. My name is Milo, what is yours?"

"Bryce Leto is the name, but everyone calls me Rice."

As they walked in the shop, Milo was stunned at all the activities that were taking place. While looking around, a man yelled at Rice and motioned for him to come. As they walked over to the man, he asked Rice who his friend was. Rice introduces Milo to Jax Abrams, the boss. Jax was medium in size and ordinary built. His eyes are the usual blue, but his squint cuts like a knife. The facial expression was faint, could be a smile or not a smile. Jax wanted to know if Milo was a runaway.

Milo laughed and said, "As of today."

Jax said to him, "Will anyone come looking for you?"

"No there is no one but me," insisted Milo.

He said, "Well then, as of today, would you like to make a run with Rice?"

Milo asked, "What is a run?"

"If you would agree, Rice will show you what a run is," said Jax. Rice and Milo proceeded out of the shop when Jax yelled again, "By the way, we will call you Lil Ice." Milo smiled at the new name and walked out of the shop. They went out to make the run, picking out a Lamborghini that had been on the target list. After getting access, they took the car back to the shop. Jax was impressed with the report that Rice gave about Lil Ice, he gave them $2,000 each.

"Wow, this is where it is going down. I will not have to sleep on the street tonight, I have green to pay my own way," exclaimed Milo.

Jax said, "Okay, then that must mean you are in, welcome to the crew, Lil Ice." Milo paused and reflected back on the moment Mrs. Queen welcomed him into the youth group. He had to get his head back to the reason he left. Rice asked Lil Ice if he wanted to go to his boy's house. He agreed because he had no other place he wanted to go back to. They left the shop, walked over, and got into an old beat up 1952 Chevy truck with no windows.

"You steal luxury cars but drive this beat up piece of junk. You are only thirteen driving without a license," Milo burst out laughing. The truck belonged to Rice's grandfather; he raised him when his mother left him on the steps of a neighbor's house. The neighbor knew who he was and took him to his grandfather. When his grandfather died, Rice went to live with his aunt. She gave his cousin the truck, in turn he gave the four by four to Rice.

Rice said, "Fixing the truck up is still on the to do list."

Milo explained, "Man, you work at a shop where they are able to fix it while you are making the runs."

He said, "Jax only does the cars we jack, you have to get your own fix somewhere else. The place is for the business at hand. I do not have time because of the runs, so I do the best I can with it."

Rice drove into the apartment complex, parked, and they went into the apartment. The living room had a designer couch and loveseat with two oriental rugs. A lamp standing in the corner by the couch with arms like a spider with three overhead bulbs. A picture window looking out onto a balcony. Four bar stools up to a counter of the kitchen. Milo pulled one of the stools out and sat on it. Rice, leaning on the counter, ordered pizza. Milo asked again if it was okay for him to be there. He assured him that it was alright, his boy would not mind. As they talked about the run of the day, his boy walked in. He began to yell at Rice for having someone in his flat when he was not around. He opened the front door and pointed for them to leave. Rice asked if they could stay till the pizza arrived, but his boy was not having it. Milo and Rice left the apartment.

Milo asked, "What about the pizza?"

Rice replied, "We will have to go somewhere else to get something to eat. Milo, do you have somewhere for us to stay for tonight?"

Milo answered, "I was living with my mother but ran away. I am without a place to lay my head."

Rice countered, "The place that we just left was my only spot to crash. Khalil was mad at me for bringing you over without permission because he has a lot of valuable items. Khalil trusts me but not anyone I hang around." Milo thought about his comfortable bed at home. Shaking his head, he put that thought out of his head quickly. He had to take revenge for the death. Milo and Rice went to get something to eat, then went to the shelter for the night.

There was a long line for intake. When they finally reached the front desk, there were two beds left. They entered the dorm area, rows of bunk beds lined in a row. Their beds were in the back of the room. One was a top bunk and the other was a single bed against the wall. Rice took the single bed to protect Milo. He put him on the top bunk to avoid anyone messing with him. They would have to step on his bed to get to him because of no ladders. As they slept, some youths took Milo out of the bed. Rice was facing the wall and did not feel the boy stepping on the cot. They took him to the bathroom area and stole all the money. Tied his hands and legs with a rope and put a cloth with duct tape across his mouth and left him there. The boys that jumped Milo were not there when the morning came; they left before anyone woke up. Rice woke and heard a mumble coming from the bathroom. He found him tied up in the shower stall. Untying him Milo let him know that they stole all the money. They now had to find a way to survive, they could not make a run till three days.

Milo at this point was afraid of being in a shelter, so they roamed the streets. They hanged around other homeless people. Some people were carrying what was left of their possessions in bags or grocery carts. Some curled up on benches, stairwells, or under bridges. The peoples stories consisted of becoming homeless because of layoffs and recessions, some physically and mentally ill, some on drugs and alcohol. As they were sitting on the benches of the library, a man in a wheelchair came, letting everyone know a truck around the corner was serving food.

As Milo and Rice rounded the corner, the truck was near a church; this brought back the reason he was out there in the first place, he had to find out how to kill someone. Being jumped in the shelter made the emotion grow deeper than ever. After eating they started looking for a spot to be able to sleep. A young man told them that if they do not want to sleep on the streets, stairwell, or bridges, they could try the woods. Milo selected the woods, it would be free from people. They walked until they came across some woods at the end of town. They entered the woods. As the boys walked to find a spot to lay down, Milo saw the angel.

Gabriel said, "Milo, I have been sent to take you home."

CHAPTER SIX

Milo looked puzzled over what Gabriel had spoken. "Take me home, I am not going anywhere with you. I have somewhere to be in three days."

Rice said, "Milo, who are you talking to? I know you have a place to be in three days."

Milo said, "I am just thinking out loud, man. I have to go take a leak and I will be back." He walked off from Rice and turned and looked at Gabriel. "Wait a minute, Rice cannot see you, can he? Are you invisible? Am I the only one that can see you?" exclaimed Milo.

Gabriel pointed out "I'm here to take you home; all will be clear to you soon. Milo, you must trust me that I know what I'm doing."

"This can't be real," said Milo.

He said to Milo, "You think I am not real, that I am just a thought." He hit Milo upside the head, who screamed out. Rice ran in the direction of the scream.

Rice asked, "Milo, are you alright, what is going on with you?"

Milo voiced, "I'm alright, a branch stuck me."

Rice said, "Keep it together. I need you all there when we do this run in a few days. If you are losing your mind, you need to go back home to your mom, dukes."

"I will do fine, you need to have no worries," insisted Milo. Rice and Milo found a place to bed.

Rice was very tired, so he went fast to sleep.

"Now do you believe that I am real, not just in your thoughts," spoke Gabriel. "The mind is the battleground for pride. Now put your pride down and let me take you home; you have to choose, this is about your destiny."

"Why should I follow you?" mumbled Milo. As he was speaking to a tree in the middle of the woods, the trunk of the tree turned purple. Milo was stunned; he could not continue to speak.

Gabriel spoke, "Now you can see that all this is for real, this is the only tree in these woods that has made a change. Let's go so you can make your change. I have an assignment to fulfill, are you ready to meet your destiny?"

"Gabriel, I will not leave Rice. I choose to stay on the path that I am on. Leave me alone, this assignment will not be fulfilled with me," said Milo. Gabriel continues to let him know that he was led to him for a reason. There were many things that will try to stop his destiny, including himself. Many forces didn't want him to fulfill his destiny, even his own decisions. He cannot choose what life deals him, but he can be an instrument in the hands of God. Milo turned his back on Gabriel and went to sleep. He left him where he was, the angel could not interfere with his will.

***

"Milo Ice, seven-years-old, is missing. Last seen wearing a two-piece red camouflage sweatpants, wearing red and white tennis shoes. Last seen walking away from Southwest middle school. If anyone has information of the whereabouts of Milo Ice, you can contact the news station. There is a $100,000 reward for the finding of this young boy," reported Jodi Springs. The reporter handed the microphone to Martha Ice.

"Please, if anyone knows the whereabouts of my son, please contact the news station or New Walk Baptist Church. If anyone has abducted him, please return him. He is only seven and he needs his mother, and his mother needs him. Milo, honey, if you see this message, I love and miss you; please come home to me." She put her hands over her eyes, and tears rolled down her cheeks. Jodi Springs took back the microphone and announced an update on the woman of New Walk Baptist Church; the perpetrator was not found. The investigators are calling it a cold case, the investigation has ended.

Martha left the reporter after hearing that Mrs. Queen's murderer has not been found and Milo is missing. Persecution has come to New Walk. Martha went back into the church. She went on with her duties, but her thoughts were on the closing of the investigation and Milo when Pastor Gavin came in. He needed the financial report for the church. He called out to her, but she did not respond. He came closer to her. When she turned around, she just started crying. Gavin put his arms around her. She moved away from him just in case someone came in with the wrong impression of the two. Martha thanked him for the comfort for just a moment. He understood where she was; he was very fond of Milo and he was praying for a safe return. He did not say anything to her because she was doing fine with no interruptions. He left her a note on her desk about the financial report. Martha could not do her best, so she went home.

***

The house seemed so empty without Milo asking her so many questions. She went into his room, sat on the bed, black head and footboard. Nightstand, two drawers with a red shade short lamp and a clock radio on top. On the left wall of the room, a black bookcase with a desk built in, the chair black and red. A rug in the middle of the floor. Martha grabbed a pillow off the bed and started to hug it tight and started crying again.

"He has been missing for twenty-four hours, I will not rest until he is found," she promised. Martha contacted the national missing person's system and other missing persons data bases, such as the national center for missing and exploited children.

She searched the hospitals, coroner's office, put up fliers, and gave information to the newspaper. Wrote blogs on the website of New Walk Baptist church. Martha let nothing stop her from searching for her son. A group from the church bonded with her and did everything possible to help search for her son. Cole, Nina, the musicians, the mimes, the praise dancers, the board had nothing to do with her and her search. Half the church bonded together in times of trouble, and the other half didn't have anything to do with someone else's troubles.

Martha did not let others' actions stop her from doing what she knew she had to do. Sitting on the bed, she had a premonition Milo was knocking on the door. She smiled and knew that he would be coming home. Martha, not knowing how or when, but he will be knocking on her door.

***

Nine years passed, Milo and Rice are still making runs. Milo has turned sixteen today, one moment he had a passion, a mentor, and a future. The next with no education and a vendetta to find his mentor's killer. From seven-years-old till now, Milo has had some kind of confrontation every day. Every situation he handled with aggression, was argumentative and hostile, whether it was good or bad. Milo battled with himself physically, spiritually, emotionally, and mentally.

Rice called out to Milo, "Come on, bro, we have a job to do."

Rice and Milo went to the next jacking consisting of four cars: McLauren Senna, Arash F Ten Hybrid Two, Mazzanti Evantra Millecavalli, and a Zenvo T. The pair had to travel to retrieve the cars. The travels took them to Italy, Germany, Great Britain, Spain, Lebanese to name a few. Rice called Jax to let him know the time that they would be arriving back. Jax was okay with the time it would give him more time to set up the next run.

Jax had high demands, and he needed them to do this run as quickly as possible. A new shipment of cars was coming in off the coastline, and this client wanted the cars whole, not just the parts. The cars were to go to a specific place instead of the shop. Since Milo and Rice were doing a great job with bringing the cars in a fast manner, Jax knew that this would be a hitch. Looking at his watch, the boys will be back in three hours. Jax called the client to tell the time of arrival.

Rice and Milo entered the shop, Jax was standing with a man who was disassembling a motor. The two walked over to Jax, who told them their next move. Rice asked when this run was supposed to take place. Jax let them know that there was a new way they would be doing business.

CHAPTER SEVEN

Milo and Rice's next run at the shipyard requires getting cars off the fleets, then taking them to a specific destination instead of coming to the chop shop. After all they had to go through to get back, he wanted them to go out again. Milo and Rice looked at each other. They told Jax about the confrontation that they had on the last run. It did not matter to Jax, and if they wanted to continue working for him, they would be going out again. The boys took the address where the shipment will be and went on their way. All these years he was doing what someone else wanted, not only that have yet to do what he ran away for.

Milo took the opportunity to ask Rice if he knew how to find someone to kill them. Rice looked puzzled but shook his head and spoke of knowing someone. Rice looked at his watch; they had some time before the pick-up. He took Milo to his cousin's house, got out of the car, and knocked on the door.

A muscular man with an apron on opened the door, "What's up, Rice? Who is this with you?"

Rice made plain, "This is Milo, my running partner, he wants to know how to kill someone."

"Well come on in, I will tell you what you need to know," said the cousin.

Rice said, "This is my cousin Knox, he will give you what you want, Milo."

Knox asked him why he wanted to kill someone. Milo explained what happened to Mrs. Queen and he's seeking revenge. Knox started talking about torture or mutilate the person, then leave them in a certain place. To gain access to a person is a trick or con, immediate attack without any verbal interaction. Surprise the person taking advantage of location, circumstances, and timing to confront. Disposing of the body by leaving it in a public place and dumping it with no concern that it will be found. Conceal it to delay the discovery, destroy physical evidence, or use time to distance the discovery of the body from any observable contact between the two.

Knox said, "You can kill and leave it as is."

Milo was quiet as they rode towards their destination. He shook his head side to side. It was a lot of information to take in. Rice reminded him to put all that he received from Knox aside until he had finished the run; he needed his head in the game, not on what he retained. As they approached the docks, Milo saw a man out of the corner of his eye crouching down behind some crates. Milo warned Rice, they thought it might be a set up. They decided to find out what his business with them was. Rice continued to walk forward while Milo doubled back to have the encounter with the man. As he approached the man, the words of Knox came to his mind. The man jumped towards him, and before Milo knew it, he had killed the man by strangulation.

Letting the man go, Milo realized he has now become a killer. Wondering why Milo was taking so long, Rice went searching for him, finding him standing over the dead man.

He said, "Milo, you carried it out, man." Milo shakily stated it just happened. Rice could not believe what he was seeing, the man was dead. They left the body where it was because it was hidden behind the crates. They continued in the direction towards the fleets.

Rice whispered, "Milo, we have a job to do, your head needs to be in place, man."

When they reached the guys that unload the cars, directions to the destinations for the cars were given out. Ryker's face was delicate but fierce with scowling eyes with a pointed nose. He wanted to know if they saw the guy crouching behind the crates. Milo and Rice looked at each other, trying not to draw attention to themselves.

He said, "I hope you two was not alarmed that we were setting you up. The man behind the crates is Nico, a homeless guy who sleeps behind the crates." Milo's mouth hung open, then closed, hoping no one saw his reaction. Dwelled on the name Nico, he had heard it before. They shook their heads and took the instructions and left.

Milo, realizing what he had done, he started to smile, "This is my trial run to what I am going to do to my mentor's killer." Milo at this moment walked with pride right along with his military stance.

***

Jax trusted Milo enough to handle more than jacking cars. The game kept changing, and the runs became more dangerous. The people they began taking cars from were dealers of all sorts: from drugs to diamond smugglers, to trafficking, you name it. Milo and Rice began using artillery on their runs. It took nothing for Milo to pull the trigger, whatever the encounter, he was ready to tackle it. Milo was no longer the little boy sitting in church, he now will kill.

The boys had their eyes on a Sweptail Rolls Royce and a Ferrari Laferrari belonging to diamond dealers. They had to wait on the instructions to tread forward; in the meanwhile, they stopped to get them something to eat. Milo and Rice were in Maldives and went to a glass restaurant under the sea. The restaurant had an impressive view, including the coral bed and marine life moving naturally around the place.

All meals are Japanese, a big difference from the beans and bread and a piece of meat in a bowl when they were on the streets. While sitting undersea, the telephone rang; it was time to go get the cars. They set out to get the instructions they were waiting on. Arriving both cars were side by side.

Milo noticed this and said, "This is strange that both cars are side by side when the owners are enemies."

Rice responded, "Shake it off, Milo, everything is going to be alright. You need to stop thinking so much. We need to just follow the instructions." Milo was slow going forth, it just did not feel right to him. As they went to pry the door, he checked it, and it was already opened. Milo backed off of the car, but Rice assured him it would be alright. Entering the cars, they drove away, taking them to the proper destination, and left Maldives quickly.

***

Arriving at the shop, no one was there as usual taking the cars apart. Calling out to Jax, the voice they heard next was from the police.

"Freeze, you are under arrest." Now Milo knew why the cars were side by side. The sign showed that the dealers pulled together to take them out of the game. The police patted them down and read them the Miranda rights. Handcuffed, then lowered their head, putting them in the car. Finishing up the raid of the chop shop, they locked up the doors and left.

***

Milo and Rice were separated at the police station, the detectives Odin West cunning with no one caring to cross his path. He was as bold as the animals in the wild and reckless as one that was wounded. His voice is as soft as honey dripping from a honeycomb. Dax Buchanan, athletic built with a strong neck in an uninterrupted unit of strength. Five feet seven, weight 178 pounds, which flowed from his torso. The detective entered the room that Milo was sitting in. West asked him if he had been read the Miranda rights. Milo shook his head up and down. The detective asked questions from the Why, Who, Whom, Whose, What, When, Which, and How. Milo would not snitch, but they had enough evidence to convict him.

Milo questioned the detective, "Detective West, has the killer of the elderly lady at New Walk Baptist church been caught?"

He answered Milo, "It became a cold case, son."

Milo held his head down on the fact that the investigation has been closed. They handcuffed him and led him to the cell until the van came to transport him to the county jail. His arraignment was scheduled for Monday. He had to spend the whole weekend in lock up. *Maybe if I would have left and went with Gabriel, my life might have turned out better than it has. I chose to stay with Rice so I could learn how to be a killer. Look at me now, a killer going to jail for something other than killing. I would have been more satisfied to have taken out the person who killed Mrs. Queen,* thought Milo.

CHAPTER EIGHT

Milo went to a Correctional Center in Butner, Rice went to a Penitentiary in Virginia. Milo was charged with first degree felony because the cars had value; he received five years for being an accomplice. Rice received twenty years. His name was tagged to stealing collector vehicles. Milo and Rice were escorted to the buses; this was the last time they saw each other. Milo was back at the starting point, looking out of the window trying to figure out what he was going to do from here. Entering into the Correctional Center, the teenagers had a lot of energy. The energy was so high like a volcano, which could erupt at any time.

The pod housed about ten inmates; the CO's did not run the house, the gangs did. Nobody dared to get on the gang's bad side, they were called savages. They were uncontrollable and didn't care to follow the rules. What was right to them is not right and what was wrong was not wrong to them. The whole environment was full of negativity. Right from the start, Milo was a target because he sat on the table in the pod. Immediately he was surrounded. Milo needed to get permission to sit at the table. Eight guys attacked him, this very moment changed his life.

Milo had to learn how to survive behind these walls. He realized that it was difficult to survive when you are alone, and everyone else is united. Fella, dark-skinned, tall, thin, and bony, hair black and curly. His face was crumbly and freckled. He was known as head of corporate. Zipper, a Latino, was the right-hand man, middle size and ordinary build foamed with rage. Cuz was next on the ladder, a short and stubby white boy but strong as an ox. General commonplace complexion, nothing to write home about, bold and brutal was his motto. The other three were just recruits. CO was officer Briggs, his eyes were unusually blue but very cold. His glance falls upon you mighty as an ax.

Fella held up his hands for the others to stop jumping on Milo. Everyone moved away from him and went over to one side of the pod. Corporate came over to Milo and explained what he required from him. He let him know that Briggs was with him; it would be useless to call on him.

"Look here, you disrespect, you will get got. Da' pain will be unbearable; in the end, you die. Yo' phone time, give me that. Yo' desserts belong to them. Ain't no diddy boppin', cuz. Are you willing?"

If you are willing, you are considered weak. Refuse, then you get jumped repeatedly. Get beat badly, they will move you to another pod. Getting moved to another pod tells that you are not with the game and it starts all over again. Milo moved to different pods because he was not willing to give in to the demands of Fella. He just fought till they got the best of him, balled up in a fetal position to protect his face and head while they kicked and stomped him. Milo did not understand why this was happening to him. The COs did nothing as Fella had mentioned, the officers were part of the game.

An extortion scheme was run by the officers, if the money was not given to them from the cigarettes, alcohol, drugs, and anything that is coming in the jail. Pain was being felt from the officers when they didn't receive their money. Nothing but corruption was going on by the inmates, warden, and the officers. Milo became aggressive, violent, and hostile. Making solitary confinement his stay to get away from the attacks. It broke him mentally, physically, and emotionally.

Milo began to lose his sanity in confinement, he began to hallucinate, which brought on anxiety and depression. He screamed out to the guards he needed a doctor, but he was ignored. He was losing all his senses, and no one came to help. He felt like a mouse in a trap, he battled every day. Milo became trapped mentally. He became a mess deep down, no longer laughing and smiling. Solitary was slowly stressing him out, along with all the fighting and abuse he endured since he got there. Once a killer on the street, now he is in a state of confusion.

He has crumbled up under the pressure; he has started to talk to himself, became distraught, despising everyone, full of malice and rage. With all of the inhumane treatment, he lost hope. Milo came to the breaking point and made a noose.

After leaving the infirmary, they put him back in the population. This is where he found out he had been in solitary a year. They continued where they left off, doing what they felt like doing. The inmates jumped him, and Milo went back to confinement. This time it drove him to psychosis where he was zoned out.

He started carrying on a whole conversation with himself. This time of confinement brought more problems for Milo, resentment has been added. He was prescribed medication with side effects that would double the effect of what he was already going through. Depression, aggression, delirium, and suicidal behavior, imagine that. Milo had a new battle to fight right along with the everyday battle of his stay at the prison.

Milo knew he had to win this battle as he survived every other battle. Taking his own life did not work, so he decided that he was going to fight to get up out of this system. Milo had to figure out a way to stabilize his mind because it is all over the place. This was the first challenge of positivity he gave himself to put away the negative thoughts that cloud out reality. Milo worked the challenge. It was difficult because of the voice distracting him. Milo made his way to the population back in the pod with Fella.

One night Milo heard a noise and looked up from his sleep. Someone was about to burn the leader of the gang in his sleep, this was an opportunity for him. He went and jumped the person that was getting ready to light up the leader, taking the flaming materials from the person. The leader woke up and saw the materials in Milo's hand. The inmate Milo jumped was the right-hand man Zipper. He told Corporate that Milo tried to burn him up in his sleep and he was trying to stop him.

Fella screamed, "Everyone, front line, no insane, no outlaw, just pure gangster. It is time to put this one here in da' casket. I told you, Milo, in the end, you die." He had sounded the alarm, but the next in rank Cuz told the leader he saw it all. Milo was the one who tried to stop Zipper and took the materials from him. What they were going to do to Milo, they did to the right-hand man instead. It just looked like he died in his sleep. Fella thanked Milo and asked him if he wanted to join. Milo said no, but he wanted him to put the word out for all to leave him alone, including the COs. Fella agreed, then started shifting ranks.

Milo did not have to fight the inmates anymore, but he still had to fight for his sanity. Still having long conversations with himself, walking as if he was still in confinement corner to corner. No one laughed or messed with him, the Corporate made sure of that. Time passed on. Milo asked Briggs how long he had been in prison? Milo had been in prison for four years and nine months. He could not believe that he had three more months to go and would be out of this place. It made it a little more better that it was almost over. He made up his mind to enroll in school for his GED. Enrolling kept his mind occupied from drifting into the dark places.

He studied hard to get his diploma. Milo was determined that he was going to make it out of here with more than some bruises, an unstable mind, scars, and having a conversation with someone that was not there. He was going to get his diploma so he could have a life outside of these walls. After all the mistreatment, Milo can now see something more than darkness. He was not going to let everything he went through stop him from this challenge to himself, not even himself. Milo buckled down and continued to do the work that was required of him to get his diploma.

Milo had nothing standing in his way to hinder him from accomplishing this one thing he knew he needed. When it was time to do the test, his mind wanted to turn negative. He had a conversation with the voice, letting it know that he was going to do this. He battled all night long with this issue; when the morning came, he was drained, but he went to take the test anyway. Milo passed the test, he received his GED. Milo accomplished all he set out to do; now the next step was his time of departure.

CHAPTER NINE

After leaving the prison, returning home, Milo realized that he had nowhere to go. He got off the greyhound and just sat at the bus station. Putting his head in his hand, reasoning about his mother, wondering if she lived in the same place; it has been years. Would she even recognize him now being twenty-one? Milo has not seen her since he was seven. How would she react towards him? Would she invite him with open arms, or would he be cast aside? So many questions that could not be answered went through Milo's head. Rising from his seated position, he took a step forward, stopping abruptly when the voice started a conversation with him.

The voice snickered, "You are not worthy to go home, your mother will not accept you because you ran away. She no longer thinks of you as her child." The voice was very convincing, the voice won the battle. Milo decided to not go home because he was not worthy, his mother would not accept him for running away. Milo heard another voice behind him telling him he must go. Milo looked around because the voice speaking now was different than the voice in his head.

"Milo, you must go home," said the voice. Milo turned toward the voice, and standing before him was the holy being. "You must go home, Milo, don't let the voices inside your head stop you from going to see your mother. You have been thinking about her off and on for a long time. Now it is time for you to put your thoughts into action. You must go home, Milo, you must go home."

"Gabriel, is that you?" asked Milo.

"Yes, it is. I have come to guide you to where you need to go next," he said.

"A guide, where were you when I was locked up for all those years?" asked Milo.

Gabriel said, "I was there, but you were not in a place to listen. The last conversation we had, you didn't want to leave the place, abandoning Rice was out of the question. Milo, you must go home." Milo took in a deep breath, he did not have anywhere else to go. He remembered the days living on the streets. That's not going to be one of his options if he could help it. The house was a few blocks from the station. Milo headed in the direction to see his mother for the first time in a long while. Slowly he walked, not knowing what to say when he saw her.

Milo asked, "Gabriel, what am I going to say to her?"

"Milo, stop worrying about what to say, just make sure you continue to go forward; don't be afraid," encouraged Gabriel. Milo still was uneasy as he approached the corner to go to his mother's house. Coming up to the residence, he gazed a minute on the house he left so long ago. The dwelling was in the middle of the circle facing out to the main street. The place with a driveway, garage, two bushes on each side of the sidewalk. The bushes nicely trimmed, Milo smiled, remembering his mother always kept the yard nice and neat. The house is brick with white shutters on the windows. He walked up to the door, looked at the bell but decided to knock instead. There was no answer on the first tap. Milo banged three times more and still no answer. He turned to walk away; halfway to the driveway, the door opened.

"How can I help you?" she said. Milo didn't turn right away, on the count that he will be seeing his mother for the first time in fourteen years. Rubbing his hands together, he slowly turned around. Seeing that it was Milo, she ran to him with open arms and gave him a kiss. Both held each other, which seemed like eternity. His mother could not believe that her son had finally come home and her prayers had been answered. She finally let him go and waved for him to come on in the house. Gabriel smiled at Milo and left. Milo and his mother walked into the house, and everything was the same as if he had never left. His mother asked if he was hungry; he shook his head, and she started preparing him a meal.

Milo asked his mother if he could go to the bathroom. She nodded, and he walked away. Entering the bathroom, he turned on the water and just stared at himself. The voice nudged him to climb out of the window, it would not matter to her. Milo started a long conversation about whether he should go or not. Gabriel appeared to remind him not to listen to the voice inside his head. To realize how much she loved him, she was in there fixing him something to eat. She did not care that he was gone, she was just glad that he was back home again.

Milo thanked Gabriel, turned the water off, and went back to the kitchen to eat. His mother wanted to know what had happened to him all these years. Milo started from the beginning when Mrs. Queen died; it had such a great impact on him. He couldn't get his head to go in the right direction. The teacher made a comment that he didn't like. He removed himself from the class and kept on walking. Trying to get his head clear to be able to return to school, he came upon a chop shop. He joined them that day and never turned back. He wanted to find the killer but only got himself deeper than he wanted to be. Finally he went to jail for five years where he was treated inhumanely. He tried to stay strong, but everything was going against him. He zoned out and now he hears voices.

The time in solitary, the torture, the fighting everyday made him angry and resentful. Paranoia sets in at times, making him offensive and in rage, he no longer trusts anyone anymore. He was stressed out feeling like he was losing his sanity, which he gave into. He decided he wanted more than what the doctors said of him being a schizophrenic and bipolar. He wanted a sense of purpose; he deserved more. He is now getting the motivation to do just that. He felt robbed of his childhood where he had to grow up fast. He did not have anything with his name attached to. He put his mind to enroll in school while in prison and came out with his GED.

After all the organized crime, after everything he went through at the hands of the inmates, he needed to make a better way for his life. He wanted to change his life because daily he saw bad things happening. He knew that there had to be some good, so he went after it.

His mother smiled and said, "I'm sorry for what you had to endure, but I will help you work out all that you need to start all over again." Martha let Milo know that his room is the same way he left it. She would get him a bed tomorrow for that one will be too small for those long legs. He had to sleep on the couch. They both laughed at that sight. Milo wanted to enter college as he promised himself; she suggested community college. When night fell, his mother opened her arms wide, and Milo went into them. She kissed him, said welcome home, son, then went to bed. Milo went towards the window and looked out into the night. As he pulled the curtains back, a bright light filled the room.

Milo whispered, "Always looking out a window; maybe if I look inside myself instead of outside, I wonder what I would find."

Gabriel said, "That's what I have been waiting to hear. Milo, I am here to give you your next step."

Milo said, "My next step?"

Gabriel said to Milo, "You are about to enter into community college, you need to major in Broadcasting Production Technology."

Milo questioned the angel, "Why should I choose this major? I have my own choice."

The heavenly being said, "It is part of your destiny. You have to face things, but all will come clear to you. There is more to come, but do not be afraid, for I will always be with you." After the angel finished talking, he left the room. Milo laid down on the couch and went to sleep peacefully. The next morning, Milo reflected on the things the celestial being had said to him. He remembered Gabriel had spoken that Broadcasting was the course he would take at the mental hospital. He smiled and went to get dressed. Milo and his mother went to get his bed as she had promised. Next they went to the community college to register him into school.

CHAPTER TEN

The lady in the admittance office let them know that orientation for that course is tomorrow and handed him the enrollment application to fill out. She will call him to let him know if he is accepted. Milo took the papers and said thank you.

The lady smiled and said welcome. He turned around and smiled at his mother. He was already in before he even got the call.

"God is good," said Martha. Leaving the college going to the car, the phone rang. On the other end was the admittance lady again, welcoming him into the college. Milo was so happy that he was accepted right away. Jumping up and down doing a dance, he had not felt this good in a long time. He had accomplished what he set his mind to do. He had the victory over his shortcomings.

***

Milo went to see the advisor; the advisor meets all her students on a personal basis. A one on one session to see if this is the course they really want to take. Milo disclosed to the advisor that when he was seven, he was inspired by the musicians and singers in church. Yes, this is what he wanted to do. The advisor was moved by what was said; she stood up and shook his hand.

"Welcome to the program, it is an honor to have you, see you Monday, Mr. Milo," said the advisor.

Tears rolled down Milo's cheeks, these were the same words his mentor said to him when she welcomed him into the youth group. He realized that this is the place that he needed to be. He left her office and grinned at her calling him mister. He rounded the corner and walked over to his mother waiting for him in the lobby. Telling her everything that happened, Martha was so proud of her son trying to put his life back together. Milo humbled himself and started a journal to get any destructive thoughts out to not hinder him from succeeding. He set his mind like a flint, it was a dream come true for him to be in the community college. This was his new life, and it felt good.

His first semester was Radio Broadcasting: putting a radio program together, mixing, demos, recording, editing, creating music, and audio/video applications. Milo became a humble spirit, not the troubled soul anymore. He became dedicated to what he wanted to accomplish. Months passed, and Milo appeared as a baby that fell down the well needing to be rescued. The voice had returned, the journaling was not helping. The angel came to give him encouragement, he needed to continue to move forward.

"For someone to survive all you went through and still standing, you can make it through this. Strength is within, so look there for what you need, you are doing well. Only have this work in your thoughts to make it to the end. Your entire world has changed. Milo, you are fighting for a place in this world and making it. Now search down in your heart and find a love for this place," inspired the divine being. Gabriel continued talking; someone who was about to come in his life to help him through the next phase of his life.

Milo probed, "Who is this person, and how will I know if it is the right person?"

The celestial explained, "You will know when the time comes, they will come when you need them the most." Gabriel left, and Milo went to class. Mrs. Olivia Lewis' skin glistened in the light, her black lashes curled over her gray eyes. She motioned for everyone to take a seat. She taught the class how to tell a story if they were on the radio. They must look at it as if talking to a blind person, describing in much detail. Everything in broadcasting was written to be spoken, so it sounds natural to the ear.

Mrs. Lewis said, "For each of you journalists, your assignment will be to write for a mass audience. If you cannot figure out what your top story will be, you can write as if you are talking to your mother telling her about something. Now, class, you can start on your assignment or you can leave if you want to. Class is over, thank you for coming, have a great day." Milo decided he would leave.

This was the first free time Milo had since he arrived on campus, he was going to make the best of it. Milo walked around the campus to see what it had to offer him. When he strolled across the street towards the grill, the most beautiful girl he had ever seen was walking towards him. As they approached each other, he introduced himself, and she added she was Leah Lee. Milo thought back about what Gabriel had said about meeting someone. He stewed over if this is who he was going to meet. His mind was flooded with the words do not forget to entertain strangers, for by doing this, some have unknowingly entertained angels. He knew that this was the person. Milo asked Leah if she had any more classes today. She shook her head. She was just heading to her car.

He said, "Well good to hear that, would you like to go get something from the grill?"

Leah answered, "Yes, that would be great, but let's eat outside. It is a lovely day." They walked into the grill, which was very crowded. Leah's suggestion was right on time, there were no seats available anyway. When they reached the counter, she ordered a chicken salad and a bottle of water. Milo ordered a cheeseburger meal with a bag of chips. They walked outside when the order was ready and made their seat on a bench under a tree. The tree gave them the shade that was much needed. This day was a hot one for Milo.

Leah asked, "Milo, what are you majoring in?"

"I'm majoring in Broadcasting, how about you?" he asked.

She said, "Psychology, much to learn, but I love to find out how the mind works." Milo became silent and his whole demeanor changed. He stared straight ahead. He could not hear Leah, only the voice in his head. He didn't carry on a conversation in her presence, not wanting her to know that he had a problem.

The voice burst out laughing, "A Psychology major, she will know that you are as crazy as you look, my brother." Leah called his name, he did not respond; she called out to him again. Milo looked at her, she wanted to know if everything was alright, did he need for her to go get help?

The voice said, "Well this is over before it gets started, my friend."

Leah inquired, "Milo, are you alright? You are scaring me."

He clarified, "Leah, I am okay, just got caught up in my thoughts. Sorry I zoned out on you."

Leah said, "It is all good, I do it myself sometimes."

He said, "Leah, I have to go. It was a nice lunch."

She suggested, "Milo, I hope this will not be the last time we have lunch because I loved the time we spent together. Here is my number, call me sometimes." Milo walked off and decided that he was not going to see her again. He left campus and went home.

***

Milo walked through the door. He went into the living room, put his books down, and turned on the television to get his homework for journalism out of the way. Milo sat down on the couch to prepare his mind to do the work. Martha walked in the living room and greeted him. He started letting her know how his day went. He spoke about the nice girl he had met.

Milo yelled, "Her name is Leah Lee, she is majoring in Psychology, she likes learning how the mind works. I do not want her to know that something is wrong with my head. I decided that I will not see her again. It is over before it even gets started." His mother looked puzzled, but she understood. Martha did not question him; she only continued to listen to him. When he finished talking, she asked what he was going to do with the rest of his day. He was going to finish his assignments for school. She asked him if he would like to go to church with her. He refused, he was not ready to step foot back into New Walk Baptist Church. Martha left it alone; when he was ready, he would come.

CHAPTER ELEVEN

Milo walked away from his mother and went to his room to get his computer. He came again and went to fix him a sandwich before he got started on his assignment. Martha left and went to church. Milo started on his homework. When Martha came back home, Milo looked at the clock, it was eight. He stopped working and decided to call Leah. The voice came with negativity, and he unquestionably changed his mind.

Gabriel appeared and said, "Milo, what you are doing is going to hurt you. What you are thinking of not going to see her anymore, and not calling because of your condition; this is not a valid reason."

Milo said, "Look, if you are not going to help me, then you can leave. I know what I am doing."

Gabriel said, "You need Leah."

Milo responded, "She is just going to want to poke around in my head, I already have many voices doing that already." He told Gabriel to leave and threw the number in the trash. Milo left his room to go look at the big screen in the living room. Martha went into his room to gather up the dirty clothing to be washed. There was paper around the trash can balled up and one piece was inside the can. She reached down and took the paper out of the can and saw that it was

Leah's number. Martha decided to hold on to the number just in case he changes his mind.

***

It has been three weeks since the last visit from Gabriel or Leah. Milo kept an eye out to not bump into Leah on campus. He was feeling good that his problem would not be found out by Leah; everything was working out in his favor. Leah, on the other hand, waited for Milo to call her; he never did. She started to look for him on campus, went to the broadcasting building but never ran into him. She asked some of the students if they knew where he lived; he was a loner, no one knew anything about him. She decided to stop looking for him. Leah let it go. If he wants to be found, he will be found. The girl turned her attention to her work, so she would not fall behind. Milo began to fight with himself mentally, emotionally, spiritually, and physically. Nevertheless peace is about to disrupt his fight with himself. He just cannot stop thinking about Leah.

Before Leah Lee, he had to fight as his life depended on it; he had nothing going for himself. Milo had to grow up and grow up fast. He knows that he must go against all odds, commit himself to the new way of doing things. He must change his life to be with Leah, but he did not know how.

Leah was a beautiful girl. Milo liked the way she smiled at him. How she held her head back when she laughed. When she talked, she always laid her hand on his arm. As he meditated about her, a smile came across his face. He wished he had not thrown the number away.

"The feelings you are having makes you feel threatened and unable to defend yourself. These feelings will make the relationship toxic. You will hurt her as you did those people in prison," said the voice.

Milo did not respond, he wanted to be with Leah and he was not going to let the voice talk him out of it again. Milo questioned himself, "Could I really be with her in this condition, would she have me?" Milo started his assignment; he had to push himself because Leah was the only thing holding his attention.

Gabriel smiled and said, "Congratulations, at least you are starting to miss her as I knew you would."

Milo said, "Long time, no see, stranger, you finally decided to come and see me?"

The angel responded, "I just came to let you know to let others in, then you will find out that there are people willing to help."

Milo said to the angel, "Yes, I am beginning to believe that's true."

The archangel said, "Good, keep it up, and it will no longer be a problem for you. Milo, you need to find a way to have compassion for others. This is a new habit that needs to be formed within you. If God can be gracious and show compassion to another, so can you, Milo." Milo wanted to know how that can happen when others have treated him so badly.

He said, "I have killed many, stole things, and taken women and children to let people do all kinds of things to them. God is the creator, He has it in Him, I do not."

Gabriel said, "Milo, you do have it in you, just remove the negativity and replace it with the positivity that is happening to you through Leah. Let the peace that is coming from her enter into you."

"Yes, I do feel calmer when I think about her," chuckled Milo.

The divine being said, "Then what are you going to do about Leah Lee?" Gabriel left him with that question to ponder on. Milo put away his books and left the study room. He made his way to the psychology building hoping she was there. As he entered the premises, the elevator doors opened and he saw Leah, still as beautiful as when he first saw her. Leah was so happy to see Milo, she ran up to him, dropped her books, and jumped into his arms. He was surprised at the action. Leah wanted to know what happened to him. She was very concerned when he did not call. His response was that he did not think she would want to be with a person like him. Leah smiled and explained if she did not want to be with him, she would not have given him her number, which he has not used yet.

She said, "Milo, you just talked yourself out of being with me?"

She hugged him again. Leah was glad that nothing had happened to him. She was fine now that he is near her again. The girl wanted to know if the lunch offer was still good. Milo nodded yes, and they went towards the grill. They sat at the same tree and talked for hours. Milo looked at the time. He had to leave and call his mother, not wanting her to worry.

Leah said, "Milo, do not let this be our last time meeting," then she walked away.

When he got home, he went into his room to get the number out of the trash can; his mother had already emptied the can. This was trash day, so the number is gone. As time went on, when you saw Milo, you saw Leah. The two went everywhere together: the movies, football games, mall, concerts, amusement park, and the zoo to name a few. Everywhere that they could think of to be together, they were there. Exam time has come, and both knew that they would have to be apart from each other to study. They said goodbye for now and went their separate ways. Milo buckled down and hit the books; he did not let anything distract him. He had to pass these exams. All the hard work paid off when he passed all his tests.

He started to call Leah but remembered he never got her number again. All this time he never thought to get it because he knew he would meet her at the spot. He decided to wait until all the exams were over and meet at the usual place under the tree. Not knowing if she was finished with her exams, he just waited everyday at the spot.

***

Milo was in the kitchen fixing himself lunch when he heard the reporter speaking of breaking news. He left the kitchen to hear what the breaking news was about. As he approached the sofa to sit down, the face of Leah was on the screen; he froze. He listened very closely to find out what happened. The reporter stated that she was raped and beaten while leaving the community college. She was left for dead behind the psychology building. Milo could not believe what he was hearing, Leah was raped and beaten, left for dead. He wondered who could have done such a thing to a sweet girl like Leah. He had to know more, but without her number, how can he find out? He started pacing the floor. His mother came into the room and asked what was wrong with him.

CHAPTER TWELVE

Milo stressing said, "Mom, the news reporter just made announcement that Leah was raped and beaten and left for dead behind the psychology building. I threw the number away and have no way of finding out any information about her. I am lost at this very moment, not knowing which hospital she is in. My head is beginning to hurt. I wish I had never thrown her number away." His mother remembered she saved the number. Martha ran to retrieve the number and gave it to him. Milo was very grateful; he made the call to her mother as she was on her way to the Regional.

Milo made it to the hospital and walked into Leah's room. He could not believe the beautiful girl was now battered and bruised. Laying there and not moving, Milo could not believe that someone would do this to Leah. As he sat with his head in his hands, Mrs. Lee turned on the news to see if they had a report on the person.

The reporter talked on a variety of topics. Milo was getting impatient with not knowing. He started to walk out of the room just when the reporter said the police had a photo of the person who fits the description. Milo turns around, and in amazement, he sees Rice's face staring at him. Milo lifted both hands and grabbed his hair.

Milo babbled, "What the! It is Rice, why would he do such a thing? The Rice I knew would not do this, he did not rape or beat woman. I need to go find him, where do I start looking? When I find him, what will I do? Rice is my best friend, he is like a brother to me."

The tormenting voice came and said, "Milo, friend or no friend, he hurt Leah. You must kill him, you can easily take Rice out. He would not be the wiser. You never found out the killer of Mrs. Queen. Now you have the chance to take revenge on Rice for what he has done to your girl. Go find him and kill him."

The voice of Mrs. Queen said, "Son, why destroy yourself, why be foolish? Find the wisdom that you need at this moment to decide what to do. That voice is the wrong voice to be listening to, remember the commitment you made to yourself. Killing is not the answer, you have to think of another way to handle this situation."

The harasser said, "You are going to listen to that, she left you, she's gone. Look at where you are now, struggling to fight for yourself. You do not need her now, you made it this far on your own. Because of her, you learned how to kill, now put it to action. You must not let this talent go to waste."

Milo's mother's voice of reason appeared, "Keep what you promised to yourself, do not fail yourself, take heed to the way you are walking. Milo, this is not the way."

The mocker came in, "You have not had to listen to her in years, why start now, my man? The last time you saw her, she was the one that dragged you to that church. If she would have let you stay home, you would not have met Mrs. Queen. And your life would have turned out better than what it is now."

Gabriel appeared, "Milo, you have your own mind, think of the right thing to do. Find your own voice; you made it this far with the fight to continue. Beaten all odds not to lose your mind; you have conquered that quest. Why do you want to let all your hard work go because of this action? Remember that you have a future, you must finish college." The offense was too great. Milo could not stop thinking of Leah, laying there all battered and bruised. Her face swollen, he hit the wall. He tried to be strong at this moment, but everything was going against him, and rage filled his heart.

Screeching Milo said, "It's not okay, everything has been taken from me, now you want me to walk away. I feel exposed, violated, very vulnerable, aggravated. I have found my voice, justice is what I am going to get." He became a train wreck.

His mother had to call the school to hold his spot. Milo went to find Rice; in his travels, a man approached him in an offensive way. He approached back, and the two started fighting. The guy cut him across the face when Milo got the best of him. He had an agenda, so he wiped the blood and kept on walking. Another dude approached him trying to rob him. When Milo refused, the guy shot at him. Milo escaped with a flesh wound.

He saw himself in a dark place. Milo said, "This is just a setback; I am just going to take one day at a time. I must find Rice, need to concentrate, and must stop thinking about what happened to me so I can make some progress." He kept on going to find his way to Rice. Milo started at the shop where they first met. The shop was no longer there; it was replaced by a bakery. He could smell the fresh bread coming from the bakery, reminding him that he had not eaten. He walked around the corner, who did he see none other than Rice getting into a Lykan Hyper sport.

Milo said, "He is still up to the old game; this is a golden opportunity. I must find out where the new shop is." As he walked, he remembered Rice's cousin. He went to Knox's house. As he was approaching the door, he heard someone call his name. Milo knew that the voice belonged to Rice. Milo froze; he had to pull himself together. As Rice walked over to him, his whole body shook. All he could think about at that moment was the swollen face of Leah. He was one that could identify with someone who experienced injustice that was inflected without a cause. He needed to find out why he did this towards Leah.

Rice said, "Lil Ice, it has been a long time since I saw you, how have you been, my bro?" asked Rice.

Milo said, "I have been doing okay, how has your life been since we last saw each other?"

Rice said, "Prison was not easy, but I made the time. They let me out early because it was crowded. We have a lot to catch up on, my dawg, come into the house. Are you hungry? There is some pizza left over that I can warm up for you."

Milo said, "Yes, my stomach is really talking to me, you will be doing me a solid." They went into the house, which gave Milo a chance to take a deep breath. He did not want anything to mess up finding out the reason why he attacked Leah. He calmed his shaking body so it would not be noticeable. Rice walked over to the fridge and took out the pizza.

Rice explained, "How many slices would you like? We have two large boxes, there was an interruption last night and we had to leave in a hurry."

Milo said, "Four slices will be okay, I am really hungry, my man, do you have any soda?"

Rice said, "Yes, there is some in the fridge."

Milo asked, "Rice, why did you have to leave in a hurry last night?" Milo could hardly wait to hear of the new game he was playing. Rice explained the reason he left was because the police were after him. He is not trying to go back to prison. He has a person at the police station looking out. She gives him a warning when they are closing in on him. The police found out Rice was at Knox's apartment and they are keeping an eye on the place.

Milo fearing said, "The police are keeping an eye out on the place. Then they can come at any time looking for you. I am not trying to go to prison either, bro, I am getting out of here."

Rice said, "Slow your roll, my man, I just told you that I have someone watching out for me. As I was saying, there are new things I am doing and would like for you to join me. I am still stealing cars; you know that is all I know how to do. The new thing is getting women to do whatever you want them to do for you." Milo thought, getting them to do whatever he wanted. He had to hold himself from jumping over the table and taking Rice out. There may be more women, and they may need to be rescued from all these injustices. He saw firsthand the pain and fear in the faces of the women and children he transferred. Maybe Jax had him take over since he was gone.

Rice continued, "There are a lot of women just walking around with barely nothing on. Showing almost every part of their body anyway, why not take what they are offering? Make them do whatever you want them to do. If they refuse, then you take it, you beat them up to scare them enough to not tell who you are. What do you think about this new thing? Does it sound like a game you would like to play?"

CHAPTER THIRTEEN

Millo's teeth clenched together, his fist were balled up under the table. He did not know how to answer him, but he had to say something fast.

"This is a lot to take in at once; it has left me without words. Bruh, how did this start?" Rice explained that he had been in and out of juvy and all he was around ever were males. He approached a woman for the first time to ask her out. She looked at him as if he was dirt. She laughed at him and walked away; he felt less than a man. Rice promised himself that no other woman was going to make him feel like that again. He was going to take whatever he wanted from them, leave them like he felt when that woman walked away from him.

Milo huffed, "Seems like to me you leave them more than how you felt when that woman walked away from you. You leave them struggling for their life."

Rice laughed, "I do not care because they do not care for the feelings of the opposite sex. They walk around with hardly anything on, inviting someone to come along and take it anyway."

"How many women have you raped, Rice?" insisted Milo.

Rice grinned and said, "Dude, in my lifetime, it has been about twenty. I told you it was something new because you did not know that this was a part of me. I have been doing this a long time. I am telling you now because I need you to watch my back as you did when we were heisting cars. And besides that, you can get some enjoyment out of it also." Rice paused for a moment with hand on his chin, then continued his conversation before Milo got a chance to chime in. He pronounced everyone he had done this, too, in detail.

Rice mentioned, "The nineteenth one was an old lady at a church, she had a Bugatti Veyron Sport. I will never forget the name of the church, New Walk Baptist Church. We had been watching that car for a long time. The problem was she was never alone." One day he went to stalk out the church; her car was the only one in the parking lot. He could have hotwired the car, but his urges wanted more. He waited till she exited the church. He followed and grabbed her around the throat. Rice proceeded with making her do what he wanted. The old lady begged him, she would do anything he wanted as long as he did not kill her. She did what he wanted, but he slit her throat when she would not give up the car. He left her naked in the parking lot of the church. Something new snapped in him; this is the reason he will always remember the name of the church. Rice had a new way of walking. He took the car to the chop shop and was paid big for that run. The next day is when he met Milo. It helped him to not do that to women anymore.

Rice was so proud of himself he had someone to look after, till he had to go back to prison. This is where the story started all over again in the next chapter. When the young man got out his urges became so intense that he went to the college and saw this young lady coming out of one of the buildings alone. He took her to the back of the dwelling and began to do all kinds of acts on her. He just went all in on her. The young lady put up a fight, and he beat her down to stop her from resisting him. She was not moving; he left her behind the building thinking she was dead. Now he was home free and no one saw him.

The next day, he saw his face on the news. After what he put on her, she will testify against him if he gets caught. Rice was not planning on getting caught; he has a mole in the police station. But if he does get caught, she will not enter the courtroom. Again he asked if Milo is playing this game. Milo could not believe what he just heard. Rice was the one who killed Mrs. Queen. He was the one who raped and beat Leah. The two people that he really cared about, this person that he cared for as a brother had taken one of them away from him. The other one's life was hanging in the balance. He could not hold back any longer. Milo jumped over the table, grabbed the knife, and held it to Rice's throat.

Milo yelled, "The old lady you raped and killed was my mentor, the young lady at the community college was my girl. You hurt two people that I cared about the most. You knew that I was looking for the person that killed my mentor and you said nothing. Now you want me to join you in hurting people, that is not an option, bro. I have seen much injustice happen to me and I refuse to play the same game on the innocent." He moved in motion to slice his laughing gear when Gabriel appeared.

The guardian said, "Milo, is this the decision that you made? You said you do not want to go back to prison; do this you will have a front row seat back to where you do not want to go. You can get justice for what you always wanted for Mrs. Queen and Leah. You have the person that hurt them both. Do not let him take anything else, including your life. The Lord is your Shepherd; you shall not want. Just as the shepherd looks after the sheep, God is looking after you, he is fighting the battle, he has placed in your hand the man that you have always been looking for, you have closure."

Milo, with the knife on Rice's throat, looked up where the angel was standing. Gabriel tried to get him to see that with this action, he would mess up his destiny.

Waving his hands in his face as if fanning a fly, he said, "Milo, you are about to go back where you were saying you didn't want to go. If you do this, that is where you will be heading. You can kiss everything you just united goodbye. The way you are feeling is understandable. Take a moment and see what you will be losing if you continue with this. You had victory over everything that came against you, so why stop now?"

Milo said, "He took the one person that ever gave me a chance in life, and he hurt the one that I care so deeply about. I am going to remove him, so he cannot hurt anyone else."

Rice thought he was talking to his cousin, struggling to speak, he grumbled, "Shoot him, man, shoot him, I can't breathe. Help me, man, he is trying to take me out. Knox, come on, man, you just going to let him handle me in your house?" Rice paused for a moment, trying to breathe.

Gabriel said, "You must listen to the reason why he is doing what he is doing. Let the man go, so you can understand the reason why."

Milo insisted, "He will get away, I will not let him go."

The divine said, "Ask Rice what happened to him when he was a child. He will not run away, he will tell you his story. He has been waiting to tell somebody for a long time."

Rice, gasping for air, said, "Knox, come on, Man, can you hear me? What is taking you so long to take him down?"

Milo said, "Rice, what happened to you when you were a child?"

Tears ran down Rice's face, "What do you mean what happened to me when I was a child?"

Milo repeated himself, "Rice, tell me what happened to you as a child."

Rice began to cry so much that he started to shake uncontrollably. Milo let him go, helped him up, sat him in a nearby chair. When he stopped crying, he told him his story. Knox molested him when he was five and still doing it. He felt less than a man being with a man. He tried to be with women, but they rejected him. He continued to be with his cousin until that feeling of being less than what he was came over him. He started going after women, taking from them instead of just asking to be with them. Every time Knox touched him, the more hostility built up in him, and he took it out on those women. Rice tried to turn himself in, but Knox always can tell that he was finding a way out and stops him every time.

Rice did not want to hurt them, he just wanted to feel like a whole man. It stopped when he met Milo, freedom had finally come for him, it was time for him to exit the pit. The dark place that he was trapped in was no more. The burden has been lifted off his shoulder. When they separated, it began all over again. He feels so ashamed of himself for what he has done to those women that it makes him sick to his stomach.

CHAPTER FOURTEEN

Rice said, "Knox does not want anyone to know that we are together in this way. If he knew that I was telling you this, he would kill the both of us. Milo, I am so sorry for what I did to your girl and that old lady at the church. I am so sorry for hurting those who were so special to you, dawg. I know how it can be for a person to be special in your life. I realize that you are that someone in my life. Thank you for coming along and rescuing me. I know that sorry does not make it right, but I am asking for your forgiveness. Milo, will you forgive me?"

Milo thought, *Is he for real? Does he really want my forgiveness after what he did to my two special ladies?*

Gabriel said, "You know what you have to do now that you know the truth behind why he did those things. Milo, remember, you already saved him once."

Milo put his head in his hands, expressing if he spoke, Rice would tell he had mental issues of his own. He shook his head back and forth, trying to grasp a hold of what was just said to him.

The voice came, "You are thinking about forgiving him, there is no room for a compassionate heart. You have been waiting for this moment for a long time. Finally you can get the chance to put to rest the man that killed your mentor and hurt Leah. Do not let this moment pass you by, don't lose your chance to get the peace of mind you have…"

Milo raised his head and looked at Rice, who still looked for an answer. Mrs. Queen, his mother, and Leah's voice of reason came. He decided to forgive him because God forgave him. They embraced each other and cried. They were interrupted when Knox came into the house. He screamed at them and wanted to know what was going on between the two of them.

Rice explained there was nothing going on, they were just glad to see each other after getting out of prison. There was nothing he needed to be worried about between the two. They were just friends and glad to see each other. Rice reminded him of the time Milo came to ask him how to kill someone. Knox ignored Rice and wanted to know if there was nothing going on between the two, why was the kitchen in a mess? Shakely Rice pointed out that he was so excited that he jumped over the counter and knocked everything over to greet him.

Milo looked at Knox and saw that he did not believe what was said to him. As Rice bent over to clean up the mess, Knox hit him in the back of the head with his gun; he started screaming at him that he was a liar and that there was something going on between the two of them. He was about to pull the trigger when Milo jumped him, giving Rice enough time to get up and take the gun away from him.

Rice demanded, "Knox, like I said at first, this is a very exciting day for me. You have come in here bringing my excitement down by accusing me of something. Now why don't you tell us what that something is?"

Knox said, "I am not going to tell him anything, how are you going to bring a stranger in the family business?"

Rice said, "Families are supposed to not hurt one another, they are supposed to protect each other. Now tell Lil Ice, or I will."

Knox shouted, "I am not going to tell him anything, it is none of his business. It is a family business, and he is not part of the family."

Rice said, "Let me explain something to you, Knox, this is my day of excitement and my day of freedom. I gave you a chance to come clean about what you have done to me. I will tell him what the family business consists of since I am the only family member that knows this business."

Knox tried to get away from Milo's grip to get to Rice before he exposed him. Rice wanted his friend to see he was telling the truth. Knox slipped out of Milo's grip and lunged out to try to stop him from telling the secret. He reached for another gun, and both started shooting. They continued shooting till they both dropped. When it was all over, Milo came out of his hiding spot to see if anyone was still alive. Knox was dead, and Rice was still hanging on. His lips were moving. Milo kneeled down to listen to him.

Rice muttered, "Now you have the facts, you now know that I was telling you the truth, my dawg."

Milo said, "I am going to call the ambulance for you, you need to go to the hospital."

Rice whispered, "No, my time is up, thank you for your forgiveness. Please tell Leah that I am sorry for what I did to her. This is my lot, and I am at peace with it. Me and Knox cannot hurt anybody else. I prefer this way instead of going back to prison and letting the pattern continue. This is my day of freedom. Thank you for saving me and being my friend. I love you, man, you are my fam." Rice died in his arms.

Milo had to get out of there before someone might have called the police; he wiped down everything he touched and looked around to see if he stepped in any blood. Everything was cleaned up concerning him and the past. Milo looked at Rice one last time, he once and for all had the closure that he set out to find a long time ago. He left the house and shut the door of his past.

***

His mother was still at church when he got home. He changed his clothes, took all the items, and burned them. The yester-years was behind him, no more Lil Ice; he can now go on with his life. Milo was sad about Rice but glad that all had ended. How would he explain to Leah that the man that did this to her, he forgave him? This turned out to be an alright day. Gabriel entered the room.

The angel said, "Milo, I am proud of you for making the right decision; everything else will work itself out. You can now live a life pleasing to yourself. Listen, Milo, there was some pizza at Knox's house. How about you looking to see if there is any here; I would love to try a piece."

Milo grinning from ear to ear said, "Is this going to be a regular occasion that you just drop in when you want to unannounced?"

Gabriel, busting a gut, said, "Will you go see if there is any pizza in the fridge? And besides you know you need me, you can't live without me." Milo smiled because he had not eaten all day. He went to see if there was any pizza in the fridge. He retrieved the box and put it in the oven, poured the heavenly messenger a drink, then gave him a bag of chips.

Milo asked, "How am I going to explain you to people? How am I going to not seem like I have lost my mind talking to you?"

Clarifying the holy being said, "If you do not want anyone to think you are crazy, you do not have to respond."

Milo thanked Gabriel for helping him to hear Rice's story. He would have never known how he really felt about him, how he protected him. From his time of birth to his last days, he saw nothing but harm. Milo made a decision that he must give back as Rice did for him, he will help a youth in trouble. The heavenly being congratulated him on the decision he had made. When he left, Milo took a deep breath, trying to relax from all that he had encountered. Leah hanging on for life, Rice and Knox dead. It all was very overwhelming, and he just needed time to breathe.

He laid down on the couch after he cleaned up the kitchen to relax. He had missed his classes, he wondered if he still had his spot at the college. He shook that away from him; he just wanted to relax. Milo turned on the news to learn more on how the reporters present the news. The meteorologist was presenting the forecast.

CHAPTER FIFTEEN

Milo's mother said, "This is a very peaceful morning; how did you sleep, Milo?" He looked up at her and held up one finger in the air. With the other hand, he covered his mouth. Pausing just enough to figure out a response for her concern. He did not want her to worry about him; he did not sleep at all. His thoughts were on Leah and what happened to Rice, trying to make sense out of all that had happened. He finished the food that was in his mouth before he spoke.

He said, "It was okay, but it was not long enough for me. I went to sleep late catching up on my assignments."

Martha said, "You have already fixed your own breakfast I see. I will just have a cup of coffee and head to the church. The pastor cannot find anything without me. What do you have planned for today?"

He said, "Since Leah has been hospitalized, I have not even stepped foot on campus. I am going over there to see if I am still a part of the college."

She said, "No need to worry about not being a part of the college. I have taken care of that for you. We have to get you a doctor's excuse. It is high time to have a physical anyway." She walked over to him and put his face in her hands. She spoke about the promises she made to herself. Whenever he came back in her life, she would make sure that she would be there for him when he needed her. She would not interfere with his decisions, but what area that he needed her, she would be there.

Martha said, "You have an appointment to see the doctor at eleven o'clock, you make sure you get an excuse for proof of your absences. You passed your exams, go get your new schedule."

She reached in her purse and gave him a printout of his grades. Martha congratulated him, then walked to the door, turned around, and blew him a kiss and mouthed love you. Milo could not believe that all he had to do was go get a doctor's note and he is still in.

Milo jumped up from the chair he was sitting at and yelled out loud. He sat back down and realized that regardless of what happened to him, he was going to be alright now. Gabriel came into view and sat across from him.

"Now you have changed the way you used to think to something more positive. Instead of looking at the hardship, you decided to look at the good things that are going on in your life. What are you having for breakfast? I heard that college students like those noodles in a cup, do you have some? Why were you yelling?" he probed.

Milo said sarcastically, "First off I have already eaten, second, we do not have noodles in a cup, and third, you being a holy being, you should know why all the excitement."

Gabriel said, "Just trying to make conversation. Where are you heading? I like to tag along?"

Milo said, "Oh no, you are not going anywhere with me; I have not learned to not respond to you if you talk to me."

Gabriel reassured Milo, "I just want to accompany you, to spend some time. I will not say anything to make you look like you have lost your mind, okay."

He fumed, "No, no, no! You will not mess this up for me. My mother made this possible for me, and I will not disappoint her again."

The archangel advised him, "You will not disappoint if you just focus on the task at hand and do not focus on me. I will just tag along like I said without saying anything to you." Milo looked at Gabriel and started to respond, but he had to start practicing not talking to him. He left him and went to get dressed. It was almost time to go to the doctor. Gabriel was watching television when he returned. Milo just shook his head.

"This is a strange angel, he is nothing like the ones that I was taught about in church."

"I know your thoughts, you will not be able to hide anything from me, my man. I will not interfere with your decisions. I am just going to coach you to stay on the right path, if it is alright with you." Milo shook his head and headed for the door. Gabriel jumped up and followed him. The cherub giggled and said, "What, no response? How long will this last? Well, since you are not responding, let us be going, the doctor awaits."

Milo said, "When are you going to start not saying anything?"

Gabriel said, "That did not take long at all, you responded before we even made it around people. I was just seeing how long it would take you to respond to me. I will not say anything more to you, I promise." After leaving the doctor's office, they headed over to the community college. Milo went to the advisor and handed her the documents he received from the doctor. The advisor gave him his schedule, and he walked out.

Milo looked at the schedule and said, "I do not have any classes today, they start tomorrow. This gives me free time to go visit Leah at the hospital." He looked at Gabriel, the holy being did not say anything as he promised.

***

Milo and Gabriel walked into Leah's room; it was empty. They turned around and went to the nurses desk. Milo asks the nurse if Leah had to go have any tests done. She expressed that Leah had died yesterday, and she asked if his name was Milo. He could not speak, he only nodded his head. Continuing she let him know that Leah's mother wanted him to call her. The nurse gave him a piece of paper that was left for him by Mrs. Lee. Milo managed to whisper a thank you to the nurse, then rotated towards the elevator. Milo held his head down, Gabriel put his hand on his shoulder to console him. Milo shook away from him.

Milo screamed at Gabriel, "You knew that this happened and did not tell me. You just came to ask for a doggone cup of noodles. Why didn't you tell me that she was gone out of my life? Why do these things keep happening to me? Everyone that I care about leaves me. Who will it be next, will it be my mother? She is all that I have left, she must be next, tell me, is she next?" Gabriel still would not talk as he promised. Milo kept on raping and raving why he would not talk to him when he's always saying something. He wanted answers from the one that comes from heaven and who has the answers to his questions. The elevator door opened, and they stepped in, and a man with no legs was inside. Milo asks the man if he was mad that he did not have any legs. The man added at first he was until he saw the fight of a young girl in physical therapy. It didn't matter what they told her to do, she did it. No matter how hard it was, she did not stop going. The young girl just kept on pushing through, and that gave him the strength to do the same.

The doors opened, and the man left the elevator. The doors closed again; Milo dwelt on the words of the man. He was beginning to relax and lean into the peace, but the grief rose up again. He caught sight of Gabriel, and before he could get a word out, a lady entered holding a blue baby blanket. The lady had been crying. Milo saw that she was holding the blanket and asked her if the baby was doing okay. She let him know that her baby boy had just died and she has found peace with his death.

Milo asked the lady, "How have you found peace when your baby is gone?" She summarized that the baby was struggling to catch his breath, the doctors did all that they could do for him. They placed him in my arms wrapped up in the blanket. She looked down at his handsome face, and he grabbed her thumb and smiled. At that moment, she found peace; with the smile on his face, she realized he was telling her he will be alright. The baby closed his eyes with the smile still on his face, and he was gone. Peace came over her entire body.

The lady said, "Thank you for listening to me, young man. I can go on with my life without holding on to the grief. I will always remember his smile. It was good to tell someone my story," said the lady. The elevator doors opened, and all three stepped out.

CHAPTER SIXTEEN

Milo walked out of the hospital confused, he could not understand these people. With the difficulties they had and they could still be alright with them. He sat down on the bench in front of the hospital. It was at first an exciting day, then in a blink of an eye, it was a disaster. His whole world has crashed once again right before his eyes.

Milo cried out to Gabriel, "Why won't you talk to me? Why has this happened to me? You told me someone would come into my life to help me, now she is gone. I opened up to her, and this has happened. My life was just beginning, the girl that I cared about is gone, what am I going to do?" A man heard him and came to sit beside him. Milo wanted the man to leave him alone, so he could get some answers from the angel.

The stranger said, "I heard you crying, are you alright?"

Milo said, "I am alright, just had to holler out." The man started to get up and leave when he felt a nudge and a cool breeze go past him. He sat back down, then turned to Milo and began to talk to him about his situation. The stranger did not know why, but he knew he had to tell him about his situation. He started with the ups of his life. He and his wife owned many television and radio stations. His wife died last year, and he lost his way. When she passed, everything died including himself. He became homeless and he did not care anymore. On one of the coldest nights, he heard a voice calling out to him, asking if his name is Ivan Watson?

He turned around to see who was talking to me. He saw a man standing a little behind him. The stranger wanted to know why he wanted to know his name. He responded if he would like to get out of the cold and sleep in a bed, then tell him if he was Ivan Watson. It was too cold to fight with him, so the stranger gave him a shot, yes, that was his name. He then explained that he still has his television and radio stations. He does not have to be out in the cold weather. His wife made sure if anything happened to him or her that the stations would still run until either of them got their heads straight. I then asked the man his name. His name was Gabriel, he came to take him back to his rightful place.

Ivan said, "Right now I am back running my businesses. I am glad Gabriel came to rescue me from myself. I do not know why I am telling you this, but I felt I needed to tell you my story. Since you are alright, I am going to leave. Here is my business card just in case you need anything, even if it is just to talk." Ivan gave Gabriel a wink and walked off. Milo put the card in his pocket.

Milo raved, "Is this why you would not speak to me? You were waiting to be introduced. I looked like an idiot talking to you, and you would not respond. Now I see it was because you were waiting for Ivan to introduce you. It was the glory you were after all along at my expense."

People started gathering around him; he ran off not wanting to have to sit through anymore stories. Gabriel ran behind him. He kept quiet as he promised him. The holy one stayed with him to make sure he continued on the path he was supposed to be on. He would not interfere with his decision. He knew when Ivan mentioned his name that it would turn him against him. Milo stopped running, he did not want to go down the old path where when something bad happened, he ran. Instead of running away this time, he veered to the place where it all began, he headed back to New Walk Baptist Church.

***

Milo went to talk to his mother about this whole situation. When he entered the church, Pastor Gavin saw him and called Milo to his office. The Pastor held his hand toward a chair for him to sit down. Going to the bookcase, he removed a lock box, opened it, and gave a package to Milo.

The pastor said, "Mrs. Queen was going to give you this upon your arrival the next day, but she died. She left this with me to give to you if anything happened to her." Milo opened the package, and she paid for him to go to a four-year college. Milo started crying, he could not believe that she gave him the choice he dreamed of. Everything else he was going through no longer mattered. As he remembered the man with no legs, the lady whose baby died, and Ivan, the man with the many stations. At this moment, he can go to a four-year college taking Broadcasting Production Technology and has a card to be able to work at the television or radio stations. All along he was being nudged to come back to the church to receive his blessing he was supposed to have gotten years ago. He now knows that what is for you is for you, and no one can take it from you. He thanked the pastor and walked out of the church. He will honor Mrs. Queen by going to a four-year college. Milo is beginning to see that good does come out of bad situations.

Milo stared blankly as he left the church. He was amazed that Mrs. Queen had such high regards for him. He could not grasp hold on to why she would give him a free ride to a four-year college. The young man could not see how he deserved it. He walked around to the youth center and stared at the building with memories flooding his head. There was a round table that they sat at. Mrs. Queen wanted everyone facing each other instead of looking at the back of someone's skull. She always started the evening with a joke. The youth leader gave everyone a chance to answer. She would laugh at the answers that were given because none would be correct. She always thanked the youth for trying.

The class studied the bible, and different games were played to try to figure out the scriptures. Milo remembered that he helped Mrs. Queen every chance he could. Maybe this is why she did what she did. A note came in the package that was written by her. He took the paper out of the package and read it. She stated she was very proud of how he took on the character of the good Samaritan. He helped her, and she wanted to reward him for all his loyalty. The woman had been doing this for a long time, and it became a routine to her, did not know how much she needed help. When Milo came to the group, he was very eager to learn. This made her look at herself. She saw that she was no longer a youth and had become an old lady.

She saw his progress that he had so much to give to others, he just needed to see it for himself. Milo had ambition, he had the fight in him to succeed. When he set his mind to something, he would go after it. When problems come his way, he will find the way out of it. Mrs. Queen thanked him for helping her to stay true to her promise to herself, congratulated him, and said she loved him. There was more after her signature. She told him it would come a time he would have to help Nico and Jade, and when it did, he needed to find it in his heart to do so. Milo folded up the letter and put it back in the package.

He breathed in deeply and let it out slowly. He didn't know how much she cared for him. He had to go tell his mother about this. His mother had just left the church when he arrived. He went back to the front of the church when the pastor was about to leave. Milo asks if he could get a ride home. The clergy agreed, and he took him home.

***

Milo entered the door of the house. Called out for his mother, "Mom, Mom, Mom, are you home. Mom, are you here?" He went all through the house looking for his mother; she was not in the house. He took out his phone when he heard the door open, "Mom, is that you?"

She said, "Yes, it is I. How are you doing?" Milo started explaining how his day went from the last time they saw each other. He did everything he needed to do for the school. Then went to the hospital and found out that Leah had died. That was a major blow to his excitement. Going out of the hospital, he encountered different people telling him about what they had gone through. The one that stuck out the most was the man whose wife died and he became homeless because of his grief. One cold night, he met head on with an angel who let him know that his wife made sure that if anything happened to any of them, the business and houses would be protected.

CHAPTER SEVENTEEN

Ivan was the owner of many television and radio stations. He gave him his card to call if he needed anything or just wanted to talk. All this was so overwhelming that it felt like his head was going to burst. Next, he went to the church to see if his mother was there, but when he got there, she was gone. The pastor called him to his office and gave him a package from Mrs. Queen. In the package was a four-year scholarship to go to college. She left a letter making known why she chose him. This was a very confusing day for Milo. He has a lot of unanswered questions and also had to make a decision for someone that has been dead for a long time. Then on top of all that, Leah's mother wants him to call her. That one he decided not to call because it hurt too much. Milo paused.

Martha asked, "Do you want to know what I have to say about what you told me, or just want me to listen to you?"

Milo gave feedback, "Yes, I would like for you to respond to what I said; you might have the answers I need."

Martha gave a reply, "I knew about the gift, the pastor tried to give to me plenty of times. I would not take it because he was the one who needed to give it to you. The man that gave you the card, call him; he is part of where you are going. You need to call Leah's mother because you were a part of her daughter's life. I know that you are hurt because of the death, but you need to call her. She would not have reached out to you if it were not important." Milo asked her if she believed in having an encounter with angels. She nodded her head. Memories came back of her experience when he told about the homeless man. She remembered her meeting with a heavenly being. Gabriel was the angel's name. She was pregnant, and her parents did not like the man she was with. They paid him off to go away from her; he took the money. When she found out about it, she did not want anything to remind her of him.

She was going to abort the baby. As she was sitting outside of an abortion clinic, Gabriel came. The message was that this child had a destiny to fulfill. She did not want to hear what he had to say, Martha did not want any parts of a man that took money over her and the child. The message again was the child had a destiny to fulfill. The holy one reminded her how she felt when she found out she was going to have a baby. Nothing mattered more to her than the child. She listened and left the clinic. There are two roads to take, the narrow way and the broad way. The wide spread way leads to ruin, the narrow way leads to life. The narrow way is where you accept the will of God. It is the guidance that helps you find your way to the narrow road.

Martha said, "Do not be mad at me about what I told you, that was just what happened in my life that I am sharing with you about decision making. I listened, and here you are, a young man having to make his own decisions of which path to take. I made the right choice, I never loved you more than the day when I thought I would never see you again. Now I know the feeling I would have felt if you were aborted. I felt like a part of me was gone forever. Which road are you going to take, Milo?" Milo happily said he would take the road that leads to life. With all the hurt, pain, hardship, and deaths, life is all that is left for him to do. He made up his mind before he left the church to bring honor to what had been presented to him. The man with no legs, the lady whose baby had died, Ivan the owner of broadcasting stations, his mother's story; every encounter pointed him to continue in his quest for his destiny. He spoke of his meetup with Gabriel and how he became angry with him after finding out about Leah. He wanted answers and he would not give them to him. Martha inquired what was the last thing the angel said before he stopped talking.

Milo mentioned that he wanted to come with him to see how his day panned out. He did not want him to come because if he responded to him, then people would think he was crazy. Gabriel promised he would not say anything. He was not going to interfere with his decisions, but he would keep him on the path he should take. The angel did just that with all of the encounters that came his way. The people were his voice when he would not speak.

The narrow road which leads to life is what he was trying to get him to see. Milo thought he was just trying to get the glory when Ivan mentioned his name. Now he has more clarity on the reason he would not answer anything he put before him. Gabriel promised him that he would not talk, and he kept his word. Milo hoped that he would show up again regardless of the way he behaved.

Martha said, "When you need him, he will show up on your behalf. He will not leave you with no direction, he will always direct you in the way you should go."

Milo asked Martha, "Do you still get encounters?"

His mother said, "When it comes down to decision making, he is always present."

Milo said, "We have unfinished business. I left in haste, not before saying some not so kind words to him."

Martha said, "You have a decision to make; when you make the decision, he will come. Whether it is the wrong or right choice, he will come, you just have to wait it out. He comes in his own timing, but he comes on time. Now you need to call Mrs. Lee, she is waiting on you."

He said, "Okay, I will call her but not right away. I have to take a shower, it has been some day."

Milo went to his room hoping that Gabriel would be there when he entered. He opened the door and looked around but did not see him. Having access to the bathroom, he turned on the water and adjusted the temp to his liking. Undressed and stepped into the shower, leaning his head forward, letting the water pound on his neck where the tension was so great. He breathed a sigh of release, the tension had left his body. Getting dressed Milo thought about calling Mrs. Lee but changed his mind. He wanted to stay relaxed; instead he looked over his syllabus. The advisor gave him an extension of the make-up work he had to do. He started on those first.

Milo started making a recording about male's cologne, voice and music tracks. He started the voice version first; he had a hard time editing his voice, he was monotone. Milo had an ear for music, that part he had no problem with. He chose a midnight instrumental mix for lovers he liked and put the music under the voice track. It took him the rest of the day to edit it. After editing he replayed the track to see if he needed to do anything else to it. The track sounded good to him; he just had to wait on the feedback of his peers. He copied the work on his flash drive and put it in his pencil case for safe keeping. He finished all his make-up work, he was now all caught up. Milo looked at the clock. It was two o'clock in the morning.

Removed himself from the chair and plopped down on the bed. He needed to get some sleep, class started at nine. Upon closing his eyes, he heard a voice.

"See you in the morning." He raised up on one elbow and scanned the room to see if Gabriel was there. He did not see anyone, therefore he laid his head back down on the pillow and went to sleep. His alarm went off at seven. He looked around the room to see if Gabriel showed up, nothing. He took a shower and dressed. He headed to the kitchen to fix something to eat. He had time before he had to be in class. His mother entered the kitchen and greeted him. Milo looked puzzled about something.

She asked, "Are you okay? You look confused about something."

Millo asked, "Did you come into my room last night and say see you in the morning?"

She said, "No, I did not. It might have been the angel; did you call Mrs. Lee?"

He said, "Not yet, I will call her after I finish my classes. I need to focus, I can't let Mrs. Queen down." Milo's mother had to go to the church. Pastor Gavin had a meeting with the building inspectors but cannot find all the papers he needs to give to them. She will pick up something to eat on the way. She told him that she loved him and will see him tonight; he responded for her to be safe. He was left alone with just his thoughts.

CHAPTER EIGHTEEN

Every single day of his life was harsh and violent. Each situation he encountered was full of hostility, aggression, and confrontation. Milo not only fought physically but also spiritually and mentally. This day he decided to let peace reign, letting go of the irritations of life. He no longer wants to behave in an irrational way. He had to change in order to give honor to his mentor. Meeting Leah showed him how to have compassion on another and how to have peace within yourself. She handled a situation in a positive way instead of a negative one. He always handled problems in a negative way, but today that changes. He can feel at this time of his life the peace flowing deep in the marrows of his bones. His mind has changed, he hoped the voices had left with the changes.

The voice spoke, "Wishful thinking, my boy, no matter the mind changes. The change must take root, and we will not let that happen for you."

Milo said, "It will take root might as well say goodbye now, for this is your last conversation with me. I will resist you, and you will have to flee from me. I am not going to pay you any attention and focus on the new way of thinking as Gabriel has suggested."

The voice started to laugh and said, "Gabriel does not know what he is talking about. Where is he anyway? He has not been around for days. Your counselor is not appearing when you need him the most. Giving you this kind of advice and not backing it up with proof. I am still here."

Milo said, "I have proof I resisted you on the day when I was making the decision to call Leah. If you left me on that day, you will leave me now, be gone. I no longer want you around me, you came unannounced anyway." He continued to let the voice know that he only comes in his times of trouble, in his weakness. Distracting him from making the necessary changes that he needed to make. Milo feared everything that happened to him; in this matter, the voices could take control over his thoughts. They were no longer welcome, he would not entertain them anymore. No more following their advice, no more having their joys on my account, the game is over.

The voice growled, "How did you find the key? No one has ever found the key but Jesus. Did Gabriel tell you what to do? It is not part of the rules, he will be judged if he gives you the key to make me flee."

Milo said proudly, "I figured it out on my own. No more talking, that would be entertaining you, conversation over. I have decided to follow heavenly counsel instead."

***

Mr. Jayce Cullen, who was his radio production teacher. His hair was long and tangled, hanging down with his eyes shining through. It was all black; so was his mustache. No color was in his face, it was white as the dead. He instructed the students to get out their projects. Only ten out of twenty-five had their projects finished. He asked who would like to go first. Milo raised his hand. He pulled out his flash drive, walked up to the television, and put it into the computer. When it was done, the class clapped and some whistled. Milo ejected his flash drive and waited for the feedback from the class. Everybody said it sounded like a real commercial. He went to sit down with a smile on his face. Today was a new beginning for his life, and he wanted to keep this feeling forever. With the feedback, he now knows that he can do anything with greatness if he keeps his mind on it.

***

Milo picked up the phone and called Mrs. Lee; he hesitated ten commenced to dial. He put the phone to his ear and waited. He began to count one...two...three...He began to pull the phone from his ear when he heard someone saying hello. Milo acknowledged himself, said how sorry he was for taking so long to get back with her. He had a hard time grasping the death of Leah. Mrs. Lee mentioned that she has her days, but she is maintaining.

Mrs. Lee discussed the topic of Rice, who brought harm to her daughter who was also dead. She was at peace knowing he would not harm anyone else. Leah would not have to fear if anyone would do that to her again. She started enlightening on why she requested for him to call her. Leah made her promise that she would help him. Leah wanted Milo to know that she loved him, she never had so much fun in her life till she met him. Mrs. Lee told him that Leah knew that he went to look for the person that did that to her. She asked her to give him her car, so that he no longer had to struggle to get to school. She needed her mother to give him all the money that she had. She began to talk about the money in the bank and in a trust fund.

She said, "Milo, I am honored to be able to give you the last wishes of my daughter. The trust fund consists of $40 million. You can get it all at once after graduation. She has over $20,000 in the bank, which you can get now. Thank you, Milo, for taking care of the situation for us. I will bring over the money to you tomorrow. What is your address?" There was silence on the other end. Mrs. Lee called out his name to see if he was still on the phone.

Milo said, "Sorry, Mrs. Lee, this is a whole lot to take in all at once."

Ms. Lee responded, "I understand. I need your address to give you the money when I close out her account."

Milo said, "My address is 555 Windley Drive. Mrs. Lee, can you explain the meaning of your statement taking care of the situation?"

She explained, "By taking out your friend for my Leah." Before he could say anything else, she gave him the time that she would be coming over. He agreed, then hung up the phone. Milo seemed to be frozen in eternity when Gabriel came over to him. He put his hand upon his shoulder and shook him. The angel let him know that it took him long enough to make the decision on the unfinished business.

Milo asked, "What took you so long to appear?"

Gabriel said, "You needed to get rid of the voices in your head stirring you the wrong way. Now that you have your attitude in check, the voices can no longer have access to you. You are free from your bondage, from old habits."

Milo said, "I now know the reason you did what you did by not talking to me. My mother explained her encounter with you. She heeded your words of not aborting me, so I could fulfill my destiny. Thank you for keeping us facing in the right direction."

Remembering what just had happened to him over the phone, Milo started jumping up and down, tears started to roll down his face. He was filled with so much joy at what Mrs. Lee spoke to him. He stopped suddenly, seeing how cold his heart had been. He started crying harder seeing how someone can have so much compassion for another. He did not in any manner know that Leah felt so deeply about him.

Milo said, "Thank you, Gabriel, for showing me that no matter the circumstances, having a cold heart will not do me any good. I know that having compassion for another can bring about change in that person's life. You showed me that in any circumstances, I can do nothing about them. It is in how I respond to them that matters. When I decided to do something in a positive way, the results were overwhelming."

The door opened, and Martha walked in the house. She greeted Milo and Gabriel.

Milo, slitting his side, said, "Thank God I am not crazy, or we both are."

Martha grinned and said, "It is good to see him again after such a long time."

He whooped, "I am glad I can talk to him around someone and not look crazy. Or is it something you forgot to tell me about generational mental illnesses?"

CHAPTER NINETEEN

Martha said, "Boy, what are you talking about? There are no mental illnesses in this family. Where are my manners, Gabriel, is there anything I can get you to eat or drink?"

Gabriel said, "Milo was just about to tell me about what Mrs. Lee spoke to him about. Anything that you would like to prepare will be fine with me, Martha." Milo explained to them that Leah wanted her mother to help him. Leah left the car, her trust fund, and all the money in her bank account.

Martha sang out, "What!"

Milo said, "Leah wanted me to have everything that she had, for me to finish what I had started becoming someone new. I can get the money in her account now. Mrs. Lee is bringing it over tomorrow, along with the car. The trust fund I will get after graduation."

His mother said, "Wow, how generous Leah was toward you, son. She had to care for you very deeply."

Milo sighed, "I should have paid her more attention. I missed the opportunity to let her know how I really felt about her. I am going to study, I must graduate just for Leah. Life is funny, one moment I was feeling really low, and this moment I feel like I'm walking on a cloud."

Gabriel said, "You have just had your encounter with peace, my boy. I will see you later, there is work I must do also. Martha, nice seeing you. I have to get a rain check on the drink, see you soon."

Gabriel left, Milo went to his room, and Martha headed to the kitchen to fix dinner. As Milo entered the room, a wave of heaviness came over him. He walked toward the bed to lay down but decided against it and started to study. He picked up his journalism book, opened it, and started reading chapter five. Looking at the words on the pages, he could not make sense of the chapter. His mind was running a mile a minute. He put the book away and went to lay down on the bed; he had to get his focus. He will not be able to obtain anything until he gets his mind clear.

Closing his eyes, he took a deep breath, blowing it out slowly. He listened to his breathing to relax himself. He let the peace fill his body on the inhale, and on the exhale, he released the heaviness. Negative thoughts clamored for his attention. He knew these would hinder him; he had to get rid of them to make room for the new knowledge he needed to get to graduate. He pushed the delete button on those negative thoughts, never to bring them up again. He only had one positive thought, and it was of Leah. He started remembering her instead of pushing her out. Milo opened up his eyes, feeling so much at peace about Leah. He now understood how the people from the hospital felt about their situation. He felt like a weight had been lifted from his shoulder; the heaviness left him. Milo looked at the clock on the nightstand. It was five o'clock.

He went to see what his mother was doing. Martha was putting the finishing touches on the dinner. Milo grabbed a bag of popcorn till everything was ready. After all that had just happened, he had to go to New Walk Baptist church. His mother would always ask him to go with her, but he always refused. Grabbing the popcorn out of the microwave, he started to pour the popcorn in a bowl when he felt the idea tugging at him. His mother had gone into the living room to watch the news. Milo waited until a commercial came on, then asked his mother when the next service was. She jumped up, not believing what he just asked her. She wanted to make sure she was hearing him correctly.

Martha repeated what he said to make sure. "Did you ask when the next church service will be? Are you planning to come to church with me, Milo?"

Milo said, "Yes, that is what I said. I think it is best. Something is pushing me toward the church. I must attend the next service. When will the next service take place?"

She said, "The next service is Sunday."

Milo said, "Okay, I will go with you Sunday. I need to go get some clothes to wear." Martha grabbed and hugged him, squeezing the life out of him. He had to tell her to let him go, or he would not be going anywhere. She let him go, and they both burst out laughing. Martha asked him why the sudden change?

Milo said, "With all of the goodness that I have come into, I need to give thanks. I have to go tell my testimony. I am not at rest and feel like I am being pushed. Maybe God is trying to tell me something and it is at New Walk where I will hear it."

She said, "I am so proud of you, son."

He said, "I need to be there, I have to give respect to this feeling. If I don't, it will seem like disrespect."

His mother said, "Train up a child in the way he should go, and when he gets old, he will not depart from it. You are older and are coming back to the place you left. You have made me happy by going to church and giving thanks for all that has been given to you." She went to give him another hug and kissed him on the forehead. He smiled at her and left to go wash his hands for dinner. After they ate dinner, they sat down to watch television for about an hour. When the movie was over, he told his mother goodnight and went into his room to start studying.

Milo picked up the journalism book; he started to read the chapter again. This time he was very focused. When he finished all his assignments, he went to take a shower. After he finished showering, he stood looking in the mirror for a long time. He could not believe how his life had changed. He smiled at the fact that someone saw him better than he saw himself. As he continued to look in the mirror, he tried to see what she saw in him. He tried to understand why she chose him? He shook his head and continued to get himself ready for bed.

He turned off the bathroom light and went into his room, put his clothes in the hamper, and got into bed. He could not go right to sleep because the light was shining through the blinds. He went over to the window and lifted the blind. He peeked out to see where the light was coming from. He looked up to the sky, the moon seemed closer than it ever had been. It was shining brightly; he had not seen such a beautiful sight other than the time he first saw Leah.

Milo mumbled, "Could this be her shining down on me to let me know that I have made the right choice by going to church? Wow! That would be wonderful to have her proud of me." Milo went to lay down again, this time he went fast to sleep. The next day, Mrs. Lee came as she said she would. Knocking on the door,

Milo opened it, and she handed him the keys to the car and the envelope with the money as she stated she would. Milo gave her a hug, and she left to keep from crying. Milo went out to the car and looked it over; the tank was full. Milo went for a ride, he just couldn't stop smiling. It was all true what was said to him. The promised words had become a reality. Everything that was told to him had now manifested. He knew now that he had to buckle down and don't let nothing stop him from receiving the much larger portion.

On Sunday morning, Milo was ready and dressed when his mother came out of the room. She was not ready yet. It was not time to go to church; she raised her hands towards him and went to fix a cup of coffee, toast, bacon, and eggs. Remembering when he was so eager about getting to the youth center, she smiled because this was his day to go and be loyal to the tugging as he was to Mrs. Queen. She asked if he had eaten, he shook his head. She saw the zeal in his eyes to go tell of the goodness that had been bestowed upon him. His mother didn't want him to lose his focus; she kept quiet and ate her breakfast. When she finished, she went to put on her clothes, and they gathered in his car and headed to New Walk Baptist Church.

***

Arriving at church, Milo parked away from the other cars in the parking lot. He saw a tree and parked near it. He put up the sun blocker and then they made their way up to the church. They were greeted by the ushers who handed them a program of the service.

CHAPTER TWENTY

As they made their way in the sanctuary to find a seat, his mother was called back to the pastor's office. Martha patted him on the arm, smiled, then walked to the front of the church and exited through a door near the pulpit. Milo looked around the temple; everything was the same as he memorized it. Thinking back on the youth group, he wondered about Jade. The music started to play, and a soloist came on the platform. When the psalmist began to sing, Milo became as he was when he was seven. He became mesmerized; at this moment, he felt real good. His life had turned a three sixty, landing back in the place he left so long ago. Tears began to roll down his face, a hand touched his shoulder.

When he looked up, an usher was holding out a box of tissue. He took a couple and thanked the girl. He did not see the name tag and didn't notice that it was Jade that gave him the tissue. She walked away and wondered if this was Milo Ice. Milo cried through the whole worship service. He could not believe himself. Milo Ice, whose heart was cold as ice, crying like a baby. He stopped another usher and asked for more tissues. Milo wiped his face just before his mother came to sit beside him. She smiled, touched his hand, seeing the redness of his eyes. As his mother took her seat, a slim gentleman with a gray three-piece suit came to the podium. He announced that it was offering time and he asked the doorkeepers to pass the buckets. The usherettes started collecting the offering, the musicians started to play, and the worship team began to sing another song.

Milo took the program out of his pocket and looked it over. He saw that the testimony service was after the offering. Milo closed the program and put it in his pocket. As the ushers were continuing collecting the offering, the musicians started to play.

One of the people of the worship team steps to the end of the platform and starts speaking, "Someone in this room is about to receive a miracle, a breakthrough, a deliverance, a healing. I do not know who you are, but you are going to hear some news that is going to blow your mind. Let us all praise the name of the Lord." The whole church started to dance, waving their hands, stomping their feet, and some moved in the aisles.

After the song was finished, the man in the gray suit came again and asked if anyone had a testimony. People began to testify of being healed, delivered, finding the one that was lost, being united with someone after years had passed.

When no one else would stand up, the man asked, "Do we have one more?" Milo began to stand up, but another started to tell his testimony.

Milo said, "Well that is it for me, I will not be able to tell of the goodness of the Lord now." He sat back down and folded his arms. The announcer thanked everyone who had spoken, then motioned for the singers to sing one more song before the pastor came.

Pastor Gavin approached the podium and said, "Welcome all that is gathered here today. This day is special, this is the time to recognize all the prodigal sons. We have been doing this for a long time. Anyone that has been going to this church, but this is your first time back in a long while, will you please come to the front of the church." People started to leave their seats, making their way to the front of the church. Milo stayed seated; he did not come forth. The pastor made one more call for the other prodigals. Milo felt that same feeling when he decided to come to church. He did not wait or think, he just moved out in the aisles and walked up to the front of the church.

Milo found a spot beside a young lady who was really shaking. He put his hands behind his back. Ten people were standing at the front of the church. Pastor Gavin welcomed them back to the church, then asked them if anyone wanted to say something. Milo took this chance to tell of his testimony. He raised his hand before the pastor finished getting his words out. Gavin pointed to him to go ahead and speak. Milo asked if it was alright to testify; he did not get the chance during service. The pastor stated only if he was considerate of others that wanted to speak. No one else wanted to speak. The clergy gave Milo the microphone.

He took a deep breath and began to speak, "Only seven at the time, Mrs. Queen's death started me on this path I am about to tell you about." Milo told about his time spent in solitary confinement and the ill treatment that he endured there.

Lastly he talked about Leah and what she did for him before she died. "One death took me from this place, then another led me back." He handed the microphone back to the pastor. There were no dry eyes in the church. The minister put away his handkerchief, reached out, and took the mic. He released everyone to go back to their seats. He asked Milo to stay a minute.

"Son, it was good that the members know how you felt about Mrs. Queen and the youth program. There has been no replacement for her since she has been gone. The board and I just last week started talking about a replacement to get it up and running again. It is good that you came today and shared your testimony. I have decided to ask you if you would like the position?"

What he said shocked Milo, tears began to roll down his face again. He murmured, "How can I take Mrs. Queen's place? I am not worthy of this honor; I left the church and everything." It was like the minister was reading his mind.

He said, "Son, I know you think just because you have been gone a long time, it is not for you to start up the youth group. Mrs. Queen asked me when she retired would I let you have the position. She showed me what kind of person you were. Studying you myself, I saw that what she said was accurate. Now I am asking you again if you would like the position." Milo looked back at his mother; she nodded her head in agreement. Turning back facing the pastor, he agreed to lead the youth group.

Gavin spoke to the members to ask if they agreed. They shouted no, they did not. Jade huffed, "After all this time, he is still taking the spotlight. How can he come back here and the pastor is just going to give him the position?" The clergy asked the visitors to take their exit, so they can discuss the disagreement. He wanted to hear everyone's reason why they are not in agreement with the wishes of the former youth leader. He started with the musicians, the minister of music spoke for them.

"I recall the last encounter we had with the lad, he did not know anything about music. When the youth have a program, he needs to plan the music for us to play. How will we be able to play if he knows nothing about music? And besides that, he is a convict. We do not need that type of person leading anything in this church. He might bring more crooks, how do we know?"

The choir director agreed with Cole. She said to the pastor, "I recollect the last meeting we had, he did not know anything about octaves. How will the youth be able to sing the songs?" The pastor listened to everyone that had a disagreement. When the last person had a chance to speak, he paused for a long time, just looking out over the people.

He began to address them to open the bible to Daniel, ninth chapter verses three through nineteen. "This is a prayer of repentance for the Israelites past sinfulness, but also of confidence about overthrowing the ones that were in the Jews way. Hindering their return to the homeland to rebuild. The years the Israelites were in captivity that time was up. Daniel confessed that they had separated themselves from the word of God. They did not listen to the prophets and separated themselves all together from God." He closed the book, looked up, and prayed for the people. He said, "Just like the Israelites, we all have done something in our lives that we have regretted. Someone showed mercy towards each one of us. Now it is time to return the favor to this young man standing in front of you. Do not take what he spoke to you about his life and use it against him. If he would not have told you his testimony, you would not have known what he went through. Do as the good book asks of us, let him come to the homeland and rebuild. Agree with me and not be separated in the wishes of the former youth leader."

The members looked around at each other and still disagreed. They shouted, "We do not want an evil doer leading anything here."

CHAPTER TWENTY-ONE

The pastor shook his head and asked Milo to come to his office after he dismissed everyone. Jade was smiling; she now had a chance to take her rightful place. Jade the youth leader has a nice ring to it. She will be running the youth center, he will have to pick her now. As the members were gathered together to talk over what had just happened, Milo walked over to his mother and asked her to come with him to the pastor's office. They walked to the front of the church while all eyes were on them. They exit the door and head to the office. The pastor closed the door behind them and offered them a seat. When he sat down, pastor Gavin showed them the documents clarifying the truth that was spoken.

He said, "This is a binding contract signed by Mrs. Queen. If it had not been for her funding the buildings, we would not have a church or a youth center. Me and your mother prayed for your return. Gabriel came to explain a vision that I had. He gave me the understanding of when you would be returning. Milo, we welcome you to finish the work she left undone."

Milo fumed, "How am I going to finish the work when these members are judging me and do not even know me? They did not even give me a chance when I was seven and still will not give me a chance. From where I am standing, they have not grown in fourteen years. I followed the nudging to come to church today. To give thanks for what was done for me. When I came into the house of

God, I was treated like I'm nothing. They shouted as they did Jesus, crucify him, crucify him! Today I know that feeling of being crucified for just being me. Pastor, there is no way that these people are going to let me do that job."

Pastor Gavin said, "It is not up to them. This is a legal document. I asked them out of courtesy. I see now that they are very unforgiving, judgmental, selfish, and a persecutor. There is a lot of work I must do in this church. I must wean out those who might bring harm to anyone that comes here to change their life. This church is about rebuilding, not tearing down."

Milo answered, "I hear you, pastor, but I am not there yet like you and Mom. These people cried for me, then turned around and started hating me. I will not bring shame to my mother because of those people. I will turn it out up in this place, starting with Cole Brady and Nina Frost. They would not give me a break when I was here before, and I see nothing has changed. Pastor, from my seat, they are not putting anything that you are preaching into action. They are just playing church. I am reading all of them. If I take the offer, you and Mom will have it hard in this church. I'm declining the proposal, to make both of your jobs easier." He rose to shake the pastor's hand and walked out of the office with his mother following him. Milo and Martha left the church. Upon reaching the car, all the windows had been smashed. He looked in the car to see if anything was missing. All the school equipment had been taken. Everything he had in the car, a video camera, a tripod, his bag with his zip drives, disks, turntable, mixing board, gone.

Seeing that he would have to replace the items, it was like fire coming out of his nostrils.

He turned to his mother and shouted, "Mom, it is on now. Gabriel tried to influence me to have compassion for others, no more compassion. I can understand this kind of behavior from those out in the world but not from those who say they are saints." Martha was in shock about the damage to the car. In no way did she want to imply that this was done by the hands of the church members. Shaking her head, she turned to Milo, trying to get him to calm down. She took her phone out of her purse, then called the police. While waiting for the dispatch, Pastor Gavin came towards the vehicle. Milo engaged in a conversation with him about the incident. Ranting on and on about his school equipment being stolen and he knows that the members did it.

The pastor suggested that they have to handle the situation in order so things can come out peacefully. Milo walked off from the pastor mumbling to himself. He stopped at a huge oak tree near the church. For the first time, he took a long look at the church. It was brick with three doors to enter in. Three windows just above the doors, also a huge clock preceding the windows, then the steeple on top. Milo glanced passed the steeple and gazed at the sky, which was clear with the sun shining brightly.

Rotating his head to the left, then to the right just in time to see a rainbow. Taking a deep breath, he realized that prayer would be appropriate right now. Not knowing where and how to begin, he twisted towards the minister but decided against it. Milo knew that a long speech would follow, and he just didn't want to talk. The police came on the grounds; he stayed near the tree, letting his mother and Gavin handle the situation.

***

Stepping back on campus, Milo felt more relaxed than he did after the episode at church. Walking in the building, there were students sitting around talking. A receptionist at the desk in the center of the room went all the way round in a circle. A staircase at the back of the room and a glass window looking out at the patio. Milo walked down the hall to his journalism class. The computer area was empty; he needed to finish up his project for his radio broadcasting class. Class did not start until another hour and a half. He chose the middle studio at the back of the room. Sitting down at the computer pressing the start button to turn it on, he began to cry.

At that very moment, he had never felt so alone. His whole body shook while he released tons of pent up emotions.

Sobbing he said, "I must pull myself together before someone walks into the room." Wiping the tears, he could feel the pit of his stomach fluttering. Trying to get his thoughts together to finish the project, he realized that it was useless because his voice would be too shaky to record now. Milo rose from his seat, left the studio, and headed for the bathroom. No one was in the room when he exited the studio. It seemed like a long walk that was only a few feet down the hall.

He entered the restroom and went to the sink. Milo looked in the mirror and started to cry again. He must get a grip on himself. He did not need to be crying in class the whole time, so he splashed water on his face. Milo heard the door open, which helped him pull it together. He walked out of the bathroom, went straight to the instructor's office. He explained what was going on while crying. The instructor understood and gave him a pass from his classes. Milo headed back out of the building, called his mother to let her know she did not have to pick him up. He decided that he would walk home very slowly. While on his way home, he spotted pastor Gavin; he was coming out of the shopping center. Milo turned around quickly, but the pastor called out to him.

He turned around so as not to be rude, walked up to him. The pastor said, "Milo, are you alright?"

Milo answered, "I am alright, just thinking about a project that I have to do." The pastor asked him if he needed a ride. Milo shook his head. He said his goodbyes and drove off.

Milo continued his journey looking for something that he had never seen before. Something that would bring his joy back, bring the smile back to his face. As he walked, he did not see anything to spark a smile. As he came to the end of the street, he tilted his head back, closed his eyes for a moment. When he opened them, he was facing the overpass. It seemed like a golden yellow light was shining brightly on it. He stared up at the sky; to his amazement, the rainbow appeared again.

Milo questioned himself, "What does this mean?"

He realized that he had to learn a little bit more about this heaven, about angel, and those principalities, all the things that he had ignored. Things that had been talked about. God, Jesus, and the Holy Spirit has now become a requirement for him. He must know what to do so he can not feel alone. He needed to know where to begin. Milo desired to know the truth behind this heaven. After speaking these words, Gabriel appeared.

The angel said to Milo, "You want to know about God? You want to know where to begin? You must believe that he is who he says he is."

CHAPTER TWENTY-TWO

The angel had another assignment to do, so he left. Moving forward Milo realized the feeling he had of being alone was no more. A smile came across his face. Now there is something that has brought joy and a smile on my face, a new start.

***

The television was on the news as always. The assignment the instructor gave was to listen to an emotional interview. The rule is for the reporter to tread carefully when the foot is on the heart. Must walk only where they have been given the right of way. This is a sensitive area of reporting; the journalist will be dealing with the person's inner self, in which the media trespasses frequently uninvited.

"Walk only where you have the right of way," said Milo. "Hmm, I have the right of way to the youth center, so I can walk in it." Milo threw that thought out quickly. He went over to the sixty-inch flat screen and turned on the recorder to capture the news footage. Moving into the kitchen, he opened the fridge to see what was left over. Pulled out the meatloaf and potatoes, heated it up in the microwave.

As he was waiting for his food, he took a look around the house; everything was matching. In the living room, the colors were red and white. The kitchen was baby blue with a country style to it with a rooster clock. The microwave dinged. He took the plate out and started to eat. By this time, his mother came into the house and spoke to him. He just raised his hand up and waved.

Martha said to Milo, "It has been a long day. I have been running around trying to find a nightstand to go in my room. Boy, my feet are calling for a soaking." She sat down at the table and took her shoes off.

Milo asked, "Would you like some leftovers?"

She answered, "Yes, thank you very much." Milo went to the fridge and took out the meal and warmed it up for her. Martha said to Milo, "Glad that you are talking; this is the most you have uttered since Sunday." He went to get her food and placed it in front of her. Milo did not respond; they ate in silence. After cleaning the kitchen, he went into the living room to start on his assignment. Martha went to soak her feet. The news report was about a young girl missing, and her parents were found dead in the home. The young girl was last seen at a birthday party. Milo found a couple of mistakes in how the reporter handled the interview. She dug the foot deeper into the heart. When he had completed the assignment, he started on the voice over he did not finish at school. It did not take long, so he studied for his English test. When he came to the end, there was nothing of urgency in the syllabus, so he laid back on the bed.

Martha hollered out to him, "Milo, Milo, Milo, come here quick." Milo jumped off the bed to go see why she was hollering; this is not her normalcy.

He said, "Mother, what is wrong?" Upon entering the room, he saw her pointing to the television. His mouth dropped open; the investigators had captured the people responsible for damaging his car.

The minister of music, the choir director, the mime dancer, and others had been caught on tape. Martha could not believe that her church family would stoop to this. She started to cry; Milo turned to get the Kleenex. He gave her the box, and she began to wipe her face.

Martha said, "I just can't believe this, I just can't believe this."

Milo tried to ease her a little and said, "Mom, it is going to be alright, the bad seeds are being plucked out of the church." The phone rang. Milo answered it. It was the inspectors on the line for them to come and claim the items of the stolen equipment. Milo put the receiver down and turned to his mother.

Before he could mention anything, she uttered, "I will not be going back to that church ever again. Milo, I know they want you to come and claim ownership of the items that were taken. After we go get your belongings, I am going to the church to let the pastor know that I will no longer belong to New Walk." Martha loved the church; this had hurt her deeply to not go back ever. Nothing or no one could ever do anything to get her to leave New Walk Baptist Church. She loved everything about it, the people, the job, the pastor, everything. But this one thing she could not tolerate. Martha didn't want to belong in a place where the members hinder a person from coming to the Lord.

***

Martha paused and gazed around the church. She took a deep breath and made her way to the pastor's office. When she opened the door, she took a step backwards. The perpetrators were sitting in the office. She asked the pastor if she could speak to him in private. Gavin asked her to sit down for a moment. Shaking her head, Martha stepped back out of the office as quickly as she went in and shut the door behind her.

The minister came out and whispered to her, "Martha, we must forgive those who ask for forgiveness."

Martha asked, "Are they in there asking for forgiveness?"

He said, "Not yet."

Martha said to the pastor, "You will have to find someone else to handle the affairs of the church. I am leaving. The keys to the church, I will bring back to you. I left them at the house. No, better yet Milo will bring the keys back to you. This is the last time I will set foot in this church."

He said, "Martha, do not be so hasty. I know that you are mad at the handling of Milo being youth leader. Come let us gather together and talk about it."

She responded, "I cannot gather with those who hinder people from coming to the Lord. That is what's wrong with me, pastor. I did my last gathering here on Sunday. It has been a journey, but this is where parting of the ways is necessary."

Pastor Gavin did not realize that it was a hindrance of coming to the Lord. Martha felt conflict was about to emerge in her; wanting to keep her dignity, she said her goodbyes and walked away from him. He called after her, but she kept on walking out of the church. Martha made it to the car with her head held high. When she entered the car, Milo drove off. Martha lowered her head and cried in silence. After a short while, she turned to him and asked him if he would return the keys for the church to Pastor Gavin. He agreed; she lowered her head again, clasped her hands together, and her mouth began to move, but nothing came out.

Milo kept on driving. He just waited till she was ready to talk to him. He looked in the mirror, and someone was sitting in the backseat. He pulled over to see who it was. Gabriel was sitting with a serious look, not his happy, go lucky self. He waited a few minutes before talking to Martha. As she took a deep breath and lifted her head back up, she turned around and looked at him. Gabriel asked

Milo to find a park with a lake. Milo drove two miles before he reached the park. He turned into the park near the pool area and continued on till they came to the bait shop. He parked the car, turned off the ignition, and waited for Gabriel to start talking. By the look on his face, this was going to be a private matter. Milo opened the door, looked around to see which direction to go into. He saw a bench facing the lake, so he walked to sit near the water.

Gabriel said to Martha, "People hurt people. They speak in a way to people that are not deserving. They treat people in inappropriate ways. People will do people dirty. Hurt wounds will come from someone that will leave a scar. Offenses will come, mistreatments will come. Joining the church does not exempt anyone from being hurt."

She said, "I understand what you are saying, but they hindered people from coming to God."

He said, "I came here today to say to you, do not let this destroy your relationship with God. Do not let these offenses and hurts hold you hostage. Let go of the anger, bitterness, and resentment, they will incarcerate you. I am not asking you to forgive them right at this moment because you have been cut deeply. At this time, forgiveness will not come instinctively. Release this pain live without the offense, then your heart will forgive." Gabriel continues to try to make her understand that offenses would come, disrespect will come, reasons for holding a grudge, reasons to be angry, even reasons to not forgive. What happens to you gives you no reason to quit on God."

CHAPTER TWENTY-THREE

"By holding on to these things, you are walking away from God, not people." He said to her that today she walked away from God because of the division and strife. That she did not have to reconcile the relationship with the people but forgive them because it benefits her. She needed to reconnect with God. Milo was getting bored looking at the people fishing. He walked around the park where there was much to see. He walked past a carousel, gymnasium, miniature golf course; he stopped under the shelter and watched the children board the train that takes them around the whole entire park.

He sat at the shelter waiting for it to come back to take a ride himself to see what all the park had to offer. He went to the concession stand to grab him a snack and waited on the train. He watched families grill out, music playing in the atmosphere. Adults were dancing, and children were playing.

Gabriel said to Martha, "The people have been exited out of your life who are not of His plan. The relationship had to break. Do not choose between people and God, let this roll off your heart. What did you lose? Nothing. You gained a whole lot, you have been blessed by this. You need to look at the hands of God in all of this. They did wrong, and you were wounded by all of this. I get all of that, but despite it all, God has been good to you, Martha."

She said to the angel, "They plotted and planned it intentionally. These were the last people who should have hurt anyone. They are supposed to be the true model of God."

He said to Martha, "Everyone in the church is not with God; they speak out of their mouths, but their hearts are far away from him. Let them know that what they did to hurt has brought true forgiveness. Pray for them that the ugliness inside be removed from them. True forgiveness is when you see them again and you do not replay the offense over again. Decide to not show this emotion to them again. Control is what you are given to the ones who hurt you. This is a movement of what God is about to do in your moment. What they did had to happen, it was part of God's plan. This will bring life to others. Take the painful moment and look at it as a movement. There is a larger story that is happening here. Recognize the movement, release the offender from the debt."

Martha said to Gabriel, "Thank you for the reminder of who I am and whom I belong to. I took my eyes off the prize and stopped running the race. I picked up the offense and left the church. This is the second time I have been deeply hurt by people that I cared about. I surely do not want to cross on the other side of the street when I see them coming. I know what I have to do." Gabriel and Martha walked the park looking for Milo. They saw him about to board the train.

Gabriel said to Milo, "Come on, my boy, there are a lot of people hurting out here. The train has pulled up, we need to gather them to come on board." Milo huffed. They walked back toward the car. Milo looked at his mother as he opened the door. She had a smile on her face; he wondered what the angel had said to get her to change her demeanor.

***

Sitting on the porch of their house, Martha pondered over what the holy being had said to her about forgiveness and to look at this as a movement. She decided to find a peaceful way to use the skills and talents of the people in the church. Milo came out and sat on the banister. Martha swatted at him with a newspaper. She motioned for him to take the seat next to her. She let him know that she had fallen away from her faith. She was mentally wounded for a moment, but Gabriel has given her an idea about a movement that needs to be addressed in the church about forgiveness.

The movement needs to be put in full force. She would not return to church until the movement is in order. Looking at the news all the time, I see what is happening locally and globally in this world. Martha asked for his help.

Milo said to his mom, "What are you talking about? What movement? I thought you said you were never going to step foot back in that church ever?"

She said to him, "Look here, young man, I know what I said. You do not have to remind me of what is already known. This is important, I feel a nudge to do this. Not knowing the outcome, I just know that I must do this. If you cannot understand, it is understandable; I do not want my project to interfere with your schooling. God will send me my help."

Milo responded to his mother, "Count me in." Martha smiled and took a drink of her lemonade. Milo poured him a glass and took cookies that were on the flowerily plate. They sat in silence, watching the children playing volleyball in the middle of the street. Everyone was home that lived in the circle, so they would not be interrupted in their play.

As they hit the ball back and forth across the net, Martha said, "Just like that ball is going back and forth, the movement has to move back and forth between the people of the church. If the people do not get it, we have to go after them so they can make it over the net. We will have to convince the board to get the movement up and running. After the announcement of you being a youth leader, we have to get some of the members on our side to stand with us."

Milo said, "After what happened, you're going to trust the members of that church?"

Martha said, "Boy, I have people that are with me in that church, not against me." She rose from her chair and went into the house. Martha went to her room to start on the movement. She took out a notepad and began to write the title: Watchfulness. What the movement was about, and how it would be presented. She sat in some of the board meetings; she can use it to her advantage. The proposal consisted of getting the members to express their talents, gifts, skills, anything that will help the church grow.

New members will be required to tell of any talent that they possess to add to the church. Once the talents and skills are known, then they will be distributed throughout the church. If there are none, then a class will be offered to find out if there is a talent or skill to display. In this matter, everyone that comes through the doors will use what is in their hands. Rather than just sit in the pews and go back to their old routines. Martha put her hand under her chin and looked pleased. She put away the notebook when the doorbell rang.

Coming into the room, she saw pastor Gavin and Milo standing at the door. He spoke to her, "Hello, Martha, I came by not for the keys or because of the work that you do for the church. When you came to tell me that you no longer will attend the church, it felt as if someone had kicked me in the stomach. I had to let you know that you mean a lot to me."

She said, "What are you saying, pastor, that I mean a lot to you?"

Gavin said, "Can we have a moment alone, if you don't mind?" Milo went into his bedroom and closed the door.

Martha said, "Okay, pastor, what are you saying that I mean a lot to you?"

Gavin said to her, "Martha, ever since I laid eyes upon you, I have been captivated by your mere presence. I did not know how to approach you. Fearing that you would think I was a pervert being a pastor wanting a relationship with his member."

Martha did not know how to respond to this. She was speechless about all these years and not knowing. There were many questions that came to her mind but decided against them. She did not want this to change what she was planning to bring to the board. Not wanting them to throw it out because of this matter.

He said to Martha, "You do not have to say anything right now. I just needed to get that burden off my chest."

She said, "I am glad you said that. We can talk about this later because I have a proposal needing to go to the board."

The pastor looked dumbfounded. He has just told her what was in his heart and all she can talk about is wanting a meeting with the board. Martha saw the look on his face and addressed the comment that he had feelings for her. She let him know there is a bigger issue that must come forth for the church to go in another direction first.

She said, "Before leaving the church, you told me to look into my heart to forgive. You need to look inside the church to see the hearts of the people."

CHAPTER TWENTY-FOUR

The church is now in the news, do you want the public to say that this church does anything to each other? I know that when the decision was made to walk out, others also left the church.

Pastor Gavin said to Martha, "Yes, there have been many who walked out when you left. Yes, there needs to be a new direction for the church to take before the doors shut for good. This came to me a year ago; you are the one the confirmation is coming through. I am glad that it came through you, Martha." She collapsed her hands together; she was so happy at this moment. The movement can come forth, this moment is working for the both of them. They can work together and really get to know each other more than being pastor and member. They both know how the board members handle proposals; it will be a breeze to convince them. Gavin said he will come by to help her to finish the proposition. She suggested they go to a restaurant or somewhere that will not bring a scandal.

He did not care about a scandal; he was getting ready to do a big sweep in the church. He mentioned that they did not bring the church into the public. It happened because a few members took things into their own hands. Seeing that half the church left with her, he asked if she could talk to them. With that great impact, she could ask them to join in on the movement. Martha shook her head in compliance with him. Pastor Gavin gave her the names of the people, then turned toward the door and left the house. Martha called out to Milo, letting him know that he had left. She picked up the phone and started calling everybody that left the church with her. Each one questioned her on why she would do anything for that church again after what had happened to her? She let them know that forgiveness is a must. Each one said they would help with the plan.

***

Pastor Gavin drove to a nearby park. He found a bench to sit on; as he was bending to take his seat, he heard his name being called. He was startled a little because his mind was on Martha. He turned around to where the voice was coming from and saw that it was Gabriel.

The pastor said to the angel, "How are you?"

He related to the pastor, "Doing well these days, Gavin. I see that you have yourself in a dilemma."

Gavin responded, "Yes, trying to find the solution to it. Martha has a proposal, and I would like to know if it will work?"

Gabriel shook his head and said, "It is part of the plan that you received in your vision last year. You have to announce that this plan will bring balance back to the church. You must express that the incident brought imbalance, and the church is being challenged. Make sure that people will want to come to God's house. The members will have to stop going through a routine of just attending church. They must do right by the new coming into the church and the prodigals and backsliders. They needed to show fairness, loving kindness, walk humbly, and not be partial. All must line up with the one lawgiver, who is able to save. Making your own laws brings chaos; they must humble themselves and not speak or do evil to one another." The pastor spoke on righteousness and justice going hand in hand. He saw the members were being unjust when they rejected Milo. When he went out in the parking lot and saw the damage to the car, he knew that they had made up their own rules. Now the church is in the public eyesight showing New Walk Baptist Church warring against each other. The church has been torn apart; half the members left, and the ones left have no order within them. Harmony has left the building, and chaos has moved in. These are the oppressors limiting people to their full potential.

These members were robbing people of their freedom because of the injustice given to them. They were not going by the standards of God. They were going by their own standards, now God has separated the good from the bad.

Gabriel said to him, "If your only concern is about injustice, then you are way off. Mercy and Grace will bring balance. Without this balance, the heart will become hardened. Mercy must be shown to those who life was not kind to. Executing true justice, having a genuine respect for others. Not oppressing anyone, nor planning evil in their hearts towards anybody. The members must be required to have remorse for their actions. This opens the way to mercy; do not block the way. Righteousness and justice must go together when you make this decision. No one but God knows the heart of another, but if mercy is shown, their lives may change for the better. The church all must be in agreement heading in the same direction. How can two people walk together, except they agree?" The pastor looked straight ahead, entertaining that this is the time for the church to go in another direction. He had to make a sweep of the people that are left. He must bring about the changes that God wants for the church. This is the time; the opportunity must not be missed.

The members should give back what has been given to them. The mannequin in the store window is dressed from head to toe calling people into the store. The church must figure out what they have on. Are they dressed to draw the people or run the people away?

The pastor said to Gabriel, "I will take a leap of faith, not knowing the outcome. I will take the risk, even if the doors of the church closes."

Gabriel responded to Gavin, "It will be beneficial to others when you do. Don't fear, or you will sink like Peter walking across the water. Walk through, the waters are standing apart on both sides of you, just like the red sea. Now, Gavin, it is time to cross over.

***

The minister drove up to the church, went to his office to meditate before he was to begin. He prayed for strength and to be able to handle what was going to come his way. Looking at the time, he went to meet with the congregation. As he came to the podium, he paused and looked out over the temple. He reached the stage and motioned for the musicians, minister of music, choir, and the director to sit in the audience today.

Gavin said, "This day is not a routine day at New Walk, there has been a change. The unknown has started for all of us. Judgment has fallen on the church because of the wickedness that has been done. Wickedness is not acceptable in this house, as long as I am the senior pastor. I will not let evil reign in this house. There has been a separation in the building to distinguish between the good soil and the bad soil. A sweeping has happened to clean out the ones that are wicked. Disorder, emptiness, and chaos is where New Walk has been reduced to. What has become chaotic has to be renewed. Disorder must be put back into order, emptiness must come into fullness. Darkness has crept into the mist. Evil and wrongdoings are abiding here amongst us. I do not want disaster and utter ruin to come because nothing is done about it. I am going to bring order back to this house.

I am chasing away the darkness to reverse the curse that has come upon this house. I am taking a stand over the wickedness and taking hold of the grace that is being offered to this dwelling. New Walk, we have a new beginning if we take it. Mercy can be established in this judgment. To continue there must be complete obedience. We have to make a shift towards the new direction. New Walk has been rerouted. Everyone must be about the Father's business. Will you take the opportunity that has been placed before us and the church?"

One member stood up and asked him, how could he stand up there and call them wicked? Another said you called us evil. One after another told their dislikes of what was said to them. They continued to yell at him, who is he to judge them? He let them finish, then asked the board if they were with him. They did not want a clergyman who thinks they are evil. Gavin looked out amongst them and saw what he had to do with these stiff neck people.

He said, "Alright then, have it your way." The congregation yelled and hollered that it will still be the same. Gavin held up his hand; silence fell in the room.

CHAPTER TWENTY-FIVE

The pastor thanked them for coming, and that this was the last day that they could enter the church. He told all of them to take their exodus. Gavin locked up the church, turned on the alarm just in case someone wanted to double back. He went to his office and sat at his desk, letting out a deep sigh. He took the risk, and now he does not have anyone left. He was not expecting this outcome. Milo, Martha, and the other half of the members went to the church to present the proposal. As they entered the parking lot, there were no cars. Martha, still having the keys, opened the door of the church. When they saw that the church was empty.

Martha, with a puzzled look on her face, said, "Where in the world is the pastor?" They went to see if he was in his office.

She opened the door, and he had his head down. He jumped up thinking the members had come back to do to him what they did to Martha and Milo. When he saw Martha, he relaxed himself.

She said to him, "Where is everyone, where are the board members?" Gavin recapped what had happened, no more board, no more members.

She started to smile, went to the door to call everyone to come into the room. When he saw the other half of the members, he began to shed tears. Then he began to laugh when he remembered Gabriel telling him it would work out for his good because he loved the Lord. They all went into the conference room. No longer having to convince a board, the pastor asked to hear the proposal. They pitched their idea; everyone was in agreement with the plan. Gavin gave them the same talking that he gave to the other members. Each one agreed to be obedient, to follow what was told for the church to do.

He said, "The church has wiped the slate clean, we are starting over, we have been spared. We will become true servants, and God will provide for us. Good will towards men will be accomplished here at New Walk Baptist Church. This is the beginning for the rest. A prayer was said of forgiveness. Pastor Gavin turned to Milo and asked him if he now will accept the position.

Milo nodded his head in agreement and said, "I will take you up on the offer since the naysayers have departed." One of the members asked what he would do if the members came back to start trouble.

Pastor Gavin took in some wind, blowing it out slowly, and said, "It will work itself out as it just did today."

***

Sitting at the table sipping on a cup of tea, Milo looked at the tag at the end of the bag. There was a saying on it: May this be the day leading to harmony, balance, and unity. He smiled, finished his tea, and went to school. Martha wondered if she should call the pastor. She could talk to him now about the two of them and in private since Milo is gone. The phone rang, picking up the phone. The voice on the other end was the man of God. He asked her if she would like to have breakfast with him. She took him up on the opportunity. Martha really wanted to get to know the pastor, see him in another view other than him being a man of the cloth.

They will meet at ten. She rummaged through her clothes. She did not want to look like she was going to church or looking desperate. Throwing everything on the bed, she matched something casual together. An orange high-waisted pant, black pumps, and a black top arms out; it was stylish and strict. Meaning strictly breakfast only. Arriving at the restaurant, Martha saw that the pastor was waiting for her. She walked over to where he was standing. Gavin let her know how beautiful she looked, and she responded likewise. They entered the restaurant; it was busy. He asked her if she would like to go somewhere else.

Martha said to Gavin, "I do not mind waiting." The host gave them a number and would call them. They stepped outside to avoid the congestion.

Martha started off the conversation with why he never approached her before now. He said to Martha, "In no way did I want to come off as a pastor making passes at the women in the church. I respect you too much, and I did not want to mess up our friendship."

Martha said to Gavin, "You never gave me a chance. You just assumed that I would call you out in front of the church or put you on the news."

He said, "No, I know you well enough that you would have told me what you had to tell me and it would have been final." They heard their number being announced and went back in the dive. They sat at a booth. The host asked what they would like to drink. Martha chose decaffeinated coffee with vanilla creamer, and Gavin asked for orange juice and black coffee.

While waiting on the server, they continued to get to know each other. When the waitress came to take their order, Martha ordered two pancakes and bacon; he ordered the meat lovers platter: sausage, bacon, and ham with two pancakes. The server left, and they let each other know that they would take things slowly and see where it would lead. Their main focus was to get the church where it needed to be. The food came, and they enjoyed their time together. When they finished eating, Gavin walked Martha to her car. He would call her later; he smiled at her, and she drove off. Turning to go to his car, the minister of music Cole walked up to him letting him know that it was not over. He and the other members will not let him get away throwing them out of the church. He showed the pastor the pictures he took of him and Martha.

He began to throw accusations about letting the members go to be with Martha. There would be action taken behind this kind of going on. Gavin tried to reason with him but with no avail. Cole turned and walked away from him. Hands fanning in the air still, talking about the evidence he has on him. The minister shook his head, this was the last thing he needed. This scandal will not be good for him, Martha, or the church. This cannot happen, it will ruin the reputation of the church and Martha. He was not concerned about his own, he could take what was coming. He just did not want her reputation to be damaged because of him.

He sat in the car for a long time considering what he was going to do. He just made a move with Martha and now this. He realizes that Cole and the others are offended by what he did. What he does not know is what they will do with the photos that were taken of him and Martha. The man of the cloth called Martha to let her know what was about to go down. Using the day that they just had, a scandal is about to revolt against the church. Martha reassured him that the day that they had was innocent. No hugging, no kissing, no sitting next to one another. There was nothing to incriminate them with.

Nothing will stop us from going forward but ourselves. They had to remember that the battle was not their own. Whoever comes against them will have a hard time taking them down; they have a heavenly back up. With Gabriel coming to give them firsthand knowledge of what to do, how can they lose this battle? He thanked her for bringing that to him. He put the leadership role in her hands for this project. Martha hung up the phone with Gavin and then called the other members, telling them to be on the lookout. They had to be ready for anything; nothing can come against the plans that have to be put into action. Knowing the people they are going up against gives them the advantage. They had to keep in mind that things may get messy. She set up a meeting for everyone to meet at the church. She texted Gavin to meet her at the church.

Milo entered the house, and she let him in on what was happening. He asked if this changes the plans that they already had.

She said to him, "No, we are just meeting to set up a plan to counteract what may happen."

He said, "They are not going to let anyone make them look bad. We have our work cut out for us."

She said, "Yes, we do, but remember we have more with us than they have with them. We have the heavenlies."

***

Everyone was there when Milo and Martha arrived at the church; they greeted each other. Gavin brought the meeting to order. He let them know that Martha would lead the project. He turned the meeting over to her.

CHAPTER TWENTY-SIX

She stood before the members and explained again about the breakfast and the pictures that Cole had taken of them. She clarified that it was an innocent breakfast. She talked about her and the pastor liking each other but will take it slow. The business of the church will come first and foremost. Martha asked if anyone had a problem with what she had said. Martha and Gavin were congratulated by the members. They wanted to know what took them so long to get together. Everyone laughed, then they carried on with the agenda at hand. One of the members stood up to ask a question. Martha acknowledged Bella.

Her long blond hair with loose curls, a few strands falling in her face. She brushed the strands from her eyes and said, "Why are they setting out to destroy you, the pastor, and the church? Church people should not behave like this."

Pastor Gavin said to Bella, "All of them are very offended because of what I said to them. They would not agree to be obedient as you all did. Wickedness and evil will not be tolerated in this house. They are plotting something against us. It is not about me, Martha, or the church. It is about losing status and position." Questions started coming, and they answered them to the best of their ability. Waiting for the war to start was going to be hard. In order to be able to go forth, they had to find out what the opposition were up to. They chose to meet every Thursday until this thing diminished.

***

Cole called up the crew, who called the choir, who called the choir director, who called the board members. All of them were to meet in Costa Rica, and everything was paid for. Everyone just needed to accept the invite. No one denied the chance for a freebie to Costa Rica. They were booked in an all-inclusive resort. Cole greeted them at the entrance of the resort. He held a meeting in one of the meeting rooms with a spa. He decided to make full use of the spa, dressed in swim shorts with palm trees long length, and stepped into the bubbling water. All eyes were on him.

Cole said, "Don't look at me like that, why waste a vacation> Now let us get on with the matter at hand. On the table is a folder filled with photos of the pastor and Martha Ice. Both have been together after she made that remarkable grand entrance to let him know that she was leaving the church. Then right after her entry, we were told to leave the church.

We must get even with them and the rest of the members that left with her; everyone has returned to the church but us. I know that her son has taken over the youth center. We must put a stop to the takeover. None of us go to the church any more, we can bring it down with no attachment to it. Rumors need to be spread about them using the media. If there are any other ways to bring destruction, now is the time to speak up." Every one threw in what would contribute to the conspiracy. When they closed out the meeting, Cole said, "Let's go take a walk around the resort to see what else we can get ourselves into."

***

Milo's attention was about Nico. He wished he knew that it was him. A feeling of sorrow came over him for taking his life. He did not know the reason why he was thinking about him after so long. He left the house to go for a walk to remove the feeling. He walked past a house with white siding. A small dog behind the fence came running full force barking. He ran alongside him till he reached the end of the fence. The dog continued to bark as Milo walked down the street. A smile came to his face that made him feel a little better. As he continued his journey, he spotted a car following him. He picked up his footsteps, and the car sped up also. He reached the corner where he entered the business section of town. Milo went into the clothing store. The clerk welcomed him into the store. Milo looked around for a while, hoping the car would be gone.

He decided to leave the store. When he went outside, the car that was following him pulled up, and the person made an introduction, saying, "Hello, Milo, you may not remember me, but my brother and I were in the same youth group as you. My name is Jade Summers. I handed you the tissue when you first came back to church." Milo eased himself. He was shaking all over. He was expecting Cole and his gang to exit the car. He reached out his hand to greet her and thanked her for the tissue.

They both smiled, and she asked if they could get together sometimes. He looked amazed at the fact that she was so forward. He agreed; they set up a time for the weekend. Milo smiled on the way back to the house, no longer feeling the sorry that tried to creep up on him. As he turned the corner, someone jumped him from behind. They hit him hard with some object that he passed out. When he woke up, he was laying on the couch of Jade Summers.

Milo mumbled to her, "What am I doing here, Jade?" She had to think of ways to let Milo know why he was in her house.

His head was still throbbing. Jade had stopped the bleeding and wrapped his head. She asked him if he wanted anything for the pain. He did not want anything but answers.

Milo said to her, "Jade, why am I at your house? The last thing I remembered was accepting your invitation for this weekend. Now how is it that I have woken up on your couch? Are you with Cole and his gang of naysayers? Do you know what happened to me? Did you see who jumped me?"

Jade said to Milo, "Slow your roll, you will know everything in a moment, Milo, just lay back and try to relax. I will give you something for the pain." She left the room. Milo was not going to take any medication from her. He needed to know why he was in her house and who had hit him. Milo tried to stand up; to no avail, he fell back down on the couch.

Jade said, "Don't seem like you are going anywhere, mister." She held out the pills, but he would not take it. She handed him some water, and he drank the water. She turned on some music to try and change the mood in the building.

Jazz filled the atmosphere. She sat across from him and waited till the medication took effect. When he fell asleep, she dragged him into a soundproof room and restrained him. She put a collar on him with a chain and bound his hands and blindfolded him. She left him in the room for days.

***

Martha was worried about Milo being missing. No one had seen him in days. She walked the path he took the day she last saw him. When she came to the clothing store, the young lady saw someone in a yellow Honda with the passenger door needing painting. Martha knew only one car like that; it belonged to Jade. She went to her job. Jade has not been to work in days. The woman called an emergency meeting. Everyone gathered at the church. Martha let them know that the battle had begun. The opposition has taken her son. They know now how Cole will handle things. They started planning their strategies to counteract them in a godly manner.

Martha asked Bella if she knew where Jade lived. She gave her the address, asking her if everything was alright.

Martha nodded her head, saying, "Just need to ask her if she would like to join us."

Bella said, "We do not even know if she is with the others."

Martha said, "No need to worry, she is not one of them." Bella walked back to the table to finish helping the others with the plan. The minister came over to ask Martha if there was anything he could do. She shook her head letting him know that everything will be alright. She will not lose him again; this was a test of her faith, and she was going to pass the test. Martha walked over to the fountain to get a drink. When she turned around, she felt a sharp pain in her head. She fell to her knees and saw a vision. Everyone rushed over, took her by the arms, and led her to a chair.

Pastor Gavin said, "Martha, do we need to call the ambulance?"

She said, "No, I just saw Milo; he is in a room with restraints, and his head is wrapped. At this moment, he is sleeping." Martha felt the peace come over her. She knew that everything was going to be alright with her son.

CHAPTER TWENTY-SEVEN

Jade walked into the tunnel that was built under the brick two-story house. She came upon the soundproof room where Milo was. The walls had white pads on them, a bed, table, and chair. She placed the tray on the desk, then walked over to Milo. Jade removed the handcuffs and blindfold. She guided him over to the table and attached the chain to a peg in the wall.

She said, "This is your food; when I return, we will have some fun." After exiting the room, Milo took the lid off the tray. Maggots fell from the plate. Gasping, he replaced the lid. Milo put his hand on his stomach, knowing this was going to be a long stay. If this is going to be part of her fun, he did not want to play these types of games. He tried to get on the bed, but the leash stopped him.

There was no bathroom. She told him she would be back, and he would have to hold on till then. Days went by, and she had not returned. His mind drifted back to isolation in prison. He had come through a lot; he was not going to let his mind get the best of him this time.

He said, "This is a test of my faith, someone will come rescue me. There is a reason why this is happening to me. When the good happens, the bad will appear to steal your joy. There is something I must do, but what?" Time and days drifted away. Milo's legs grew numb from being in the chair. He did some exercise to keep the circulation going in his legs. He did everything he could think of to keep his sanity. Day by day, he grew weaker. He did not even have any strength to keep the circulation going in his legs. He started to give up and give in, he had no more fight in him.

The voice said, "Well, my boy, that fight did not last long. I knew you could not bet the champion. I got you...." Gabriel appeared.

He said, "This is time for war, Milo, you must fight what has come against you. I have given you the strength to do it."

He said, "I am not able to fight this battle, there is nothing left in me to fight."

The angel said, "You know what to do, remember how you made it through all the other times you have been trapped."

The voice spoke, "How are you going to come up in here and try to stop my show, Gabriel?"

Gabriel said, "This battle is already won, he has the victory over you."

The voice said, "We will see about that."

Milo thought of all the times he had been in a difficult situation. Then with making the right decisions, he came out with more than enough to keep him going. He received strength from Gabriel. The voice left out screaming mad. The door of the room opened, and Jade walked in. Not knowing that he had strength, she started unlocking the leash. She turned to get the bag that she had brought in the room. When this occurred, Milo took off the collar and put it around her neck and locked it as he was prior. She could not believe that he was strong after so many weeks with no food and drink. She wondered where the strength came from. Milo wanted to know why she did this to him.

She started at the point when they were in the youth group together. "Mrs. Queen idolized you, the rest of us kids were overlooked. Our talents were not favored as yours was. When Mrs. Queen died, we were glad because now our talents would get noticed. It did not happen, they closed the youth center. All the youth left the church; she was the only child that stayed around. Her brother had gotten mixed up with a bad crowd going from city to city. He formed a habit he could not break. The people stopped him from being with them because of his habit. He became homeless living on the docks behind some crates. The owner of the docks let him stay because he was harmless. He died on the docks; the killer was never found."

She said, "They did not find the person who killed my brother. Me and you know who killed him, isn't that right, Milo?" He could not believe what he was hearing. The past keeps coming back to confront him. All this was happening because of the man he killed while stealing cars.

He said, "What do you mean, me and you know who killed him?"

She replied, "I saw you at church and thought about my brother. Came home looking through the little bit of things he had left in life. I came across a notepad that he had scribbled your name in blood. I need to know why you killed my brother?" He was wondering how he was going to get her to forgive him. This was going to be a hard task seeing that she had already tortured him.

Milo said, "Jade, me and my boy Rice were doing a run. We thought we were being set up, I saw someone behind the crates. We circled around, and I found him. He launched at me with a knife to take my money, I killed him in self-defense. Jade, I cannot do anything about how the youth teacher acted. All I can say about your brother is that I am sorry. I left the church to seek revenge on the one that killed Mrs. Queen. What happened to your brother was self defense. He kept trying to reach for my money, and I strangled him, not to kill him, just to get him off of me."

She said, "Why did you just leave him there if you did not mean to kill him and if it was self-defense?"

He said, "I was scared; I listened to my friend instead of my heart. He was the one I found out later, who killed our youth leader and my girlfriend."

Milo continued to try and convince her that what was done, neither of them could change it. What they can do is work together and change what is happening now. He forgave her for the torture, then asked her if she would like to help with the youths that he will be mentoring. He wanted to see the talents that she had. She agreed, and he let her go. All was forgiven for what happened to her brother; another door has closed on his past. The battle was turned, and he received the victory. It was a terrible situation, but he stood strong. His attitude was kept in a positive mode during the whole circumstance. What he demonstrated was a powerful determination, and grace was put into action.

Great offenses have to be laid to rest. Defeat came, but he did not leave his post. Jade laid the great offense to rest with calmness. Grace made it easy for him to receive forgiveness. He did not let the voice limit him from reaching the destination he required. The situation tried to take the life out of him, but he guarded his heart. There was a stumble, a struggle, even a fall, but his actions were of divine might.

He was a conqueror; the offense was forgiven. His faith was tried in the fire, now he has increased. Milo has grown into maturity, he made the right decision. He took action by choosing life, not death. It is now time for them both to go forward.

Milo has officially put away the confrontation, arguing, aggression, and the hostility towards people. He has taken hold to compassion once again. The chapter of this life has come to an end peacefully. Love, harmony, and order has taken their place. A change of heart, his life has taken on a new meaning. His mind has arrived at a balanced state. He realizes that he has moved forward into better days. He wanted to enjoy life, a fresh start. He has come to a level of excellence; he now is looking like the masterpiece that he was made to be. Milo has cultivated what is inside of him. He is the marksman who has hit the target with great precision. He has kicked into another gear finding joy, finding life. Both of them found new ways of thinking, new perspectives, they have matured emotionally.

They are both launching out in the deep for a huge catch of fish, they have become fishermen. Milo and Jade are in a moment of glory. No ill feelings, they have been exchanged with love. The hearts of stone for both have been rolled away. In this moment, a difference has been made. The war has ended, and the healing has begun. They have connected to opportunity, investing in themselves to take the next shot to grow. Jade and Milo have stepped into the unknown, to sharpen their skills and talents. Stirring up the excellence inside, they have accepted the call to action. The process has begun, it has been measured, seasoned, tempered, and perfected.

***

Martha looks around her bedroom, seeing if changes can be made. Gabriel appeared. He went to sit in the recliner by the window. Martha wanted to know if anything had happened to Milo for his appearance at this time.

CHAPTER
TWENTY-EIGHT

Gabriel said, "Martha, you have forgiven those who had hurt you and Milo. You let me set things right, your loved one will return to you. When he has returned, he has a job to do that you cannot interfere with. Suffer it to be, so that these words can be fulfilled. He will have to minister to the people who harbor unforgiveness. The people who are burdened down with misery and guilt are overflowing with rage and resentment. Hostility is the wall that has enclosed them; they will not let anyone scale it. Unforgiveness defiles those who bear it. He will be fruitful and multiply by assembling the people for the church. Their soul has been destroyed because of ill will. He has to love the unlovable.

The people will try to put him in a trap. They will be dealt with because he is innocent. He has not held a pity party or a poor little me memorial. He has not held on to any offenses or hurts. The young man has laid aside the weights. He is focusing on forgiving the past and looking towards what lies ahead. He is being meek and humbled, now he has to show others how to. He stood through the trials and tribulations at the hands of others.

Milo is called to be the one to calm the storm that is raging. He is the one who must speak peace into the midst of the thunder and lighting. Martha, the more frustrating the environment, the more fruitful you will become. Be about the business at hand, do not waste time. Milo Ice will change lives, this is true victory. His heart will soar because of it. He will be the one who comforts the suffering, speaks to the people in all kinds of conditions. The boy will be as bold as a lion, he needs to press his way into the direction that is being given.

Martha, your role is of service, not to fight about who is the greatest. You started the project, but Milo will finish it. You will reap the benefits of being a wise, victorious woman. Milo has a different countenance to receive what is coming next. He will go above and beyond to reach the top.

Walk in love, and the head of the giant will be cut off. His suffering has revealed the foundation that his life was built on. The angles are descending and ascending, dominion will rule the situation. You are now free to love Gavin in this beautiful place."

***

Pastor Gavin, walking around the campus of the church praying, entered the youth center, which he had not been in since the death of the youth leader. He put up a petition over the new start of the center and the ones that will be entering the building. He left the building and walked into the church. He made supplications for the new people that would be coming into the sanctuary. Gavin finished communing with God. He went into his office, sat down, and started working on some unfinished business of the church.

Not able to concentrate, he said, "I have to do the best I can to get this church back up and running like it is supposed to be. I will let nothing or no one stand in the way of the proposal. The plan must go forth; as the leader of this house, it is my responsibility to see this through."

Gabriel said to Gavin, "I am glad you said that. By letting the toxic people go and not letting the evil spread here. You will receive what you are asking for. Instead of not having anyone to fill the place, you will receive the increase, the overflow, the abundance. You have people around you that are willing to help you, not hurt you to rebuild. Those who will fill the place will bring development, not drainage. They will exalt, not exhaust. Pastor Gavin, you made a discernment about the people around you. These people had history but not destiny. No more delays or limitations, a turnaround has happened for New Walk. Do not fear, Gavin; this is concerning the future of the church. You are wearing the armor of God. You have fed the sheep, so do not be afraid of what has come against you. They have heard what God requires of them through the words you preached. They have defiled you, Martha, and the church; fight the battle, you will win."

Gabriel said, "You always fought your battles in secret and have proof that God is with you. God was with you when you started pastoring. He was there when the people filled the place, he was there when the neighbors did not want a church here. Now God will show up in the open. People will know that he is who he says he is. You must be about this business that is in front of you. You must not waste any more time. Gavin, you must follow through to what is coming next. You must know that this will change a whole lot of people's lives. True victory is here, the Lord is touching your heart, you will soar. Will you put your trust in him and believe that he is? If you rely on the one who has already proven himself, no need to be afraid of the challenge you are facing. Take out the rock and sling, go with the weapons that are proven for victory. You have been mocked, and the tortures will have a haughty fall. They will see the protector come through. Cole underestimated you, Pastor, he saw you as a pushover. If God is for you, who can be against you? The weapons that they use against you, Martha and the church will be used against them. The finger that is pointing at you will turn and point back at the accusers. Nothing else will come against the church."

***

After bathing Milo and Jade went to a soul food restaurant to get him a proper meal to eat. A sign was there for them to just have a seat. Taking a booth, a slim man came over and asked them if they were ready to order or if they needed a moment. They asked for sweet tea and lemons on the side. Milo reached for the menus to see what the specials were for today. While waiting on the waiter, Martha walked in and spotted the both of them. She ran over, pulled Milo up, and gave him a hug. She held him tight and would not let him go. He asked to be let loose; she hesitated but released her grasped upon him.

Martha wanted to know everything; as Milo was beginning to talk, the waiter came to take their order. His mother wanted lemonade, steak, potatoes, and collard greens. Milo ordered baked spaghetti with a salad. Jade asked for the meatloaf special. The waiter thanked them and walked away.

Martha said to Milo, "I want to know where have you been all this time. I took care of your schooling, but I need you to explain to me everything right now. Where have you been all this time; look like you have lost weight, what happened to you?"

Milo said to her, "Mother, I will tell you everything later; let us enjoy each other at this time please. I am hungry and all I want to do currently is eat. If you wouldn't mind, let us eat first, then everything else will be told later." Jade sat with her hands folded, looking out of the picture window while watching a bird flying back and forth from limb to limb. She hoped Milo wouldn't let his mother know that she held him as a hostage. Martha always had high esteem for her. She always treated her with respect, and to do this to her son, what would she think of her now? If he tells her what happened, things will change between her and Martha.

The place was not busy, the food did not take long to prepare. When every plate was placed on the table, Milo dived in quickly and did not look up till he was finished. Martha wanted to say something but decided against it. When he finished, he asked the waiter for another plate. Martha patiently waited for the answers to her questions. Her phone rang; she answered it and told the person she will be there in about an hour. She turned to Jade and asked if she would like to help them with the plan of getting the community to join the church. If her answer is yes, she would have to talk to the pastor to see if she would agree to be obedient with the process for the church members.

Jade did not know how to answer her because if Milo tells her the events of what she did, that will spoil everything. Milo sees the hesitation and begins to speak on some of what happened to put her at ease.

CHAPTER TWENTY-NINE

Milo said to his mother, "Jade invited me over to her house. She was so kind to hand me tissues the day of my return back to church. We talked about being in the youth group together. Sorry I did not call you, but she was feeling sad about her brother. We had to take the trip to the place where he was killed. All has been resolved; she now feels peace and forgiveness about his death." Martha reflected back on what Gabriel had said to her about he will have to speak to the people. She was glad that all was at rest, that everything was alright. She did not mention that she saw him in a room bond with his head bandage. If this was the story he was going to tell, then she would have to accept it.

Milo must have a good reason not to tell her the truth. He never lied to her before now. Jade could not believe what had just happened. How gracious he was toward her with his mother. She could not understand the reason why he did not give her away just now. When they completed their meal, Martha asked them if they would like to go to the church for a meeting. Milo and Jade came on one accord with Martha. Jade squeezed Milo's hand as they left the restaurant. The young man smiled at her as she mouthed thank you to him. They rode to church together. Martha wanted him close to her, but she gave him his space.

His mother stood for a few minutes watching them drive away. Wanting to know what they are up to. What is going on between him and Jade? He never lied to her before, why now? Would she have to cover for him again? Would he finish college now that he met her? So many thoughts flooded her head. She pushed them aside to focus on what she was about to face.

***

Gathering at the meeting hall, everyone was present, except Gavin. Entering the double doors into the spacious room with a board table with twenty high back chairs, there was a glass window to see in and out of the room to a gorgeous flower bed leading up to a gazebo.

In the lefthand corner of the area was a table with coffee and donuts. Martha opened the meeting by greeting everyone. She started the planning process of gathering the community for fun and activities. When she was finished, she asked if anyone had anything else to add. At that time, Pastor Gavin walked into the meeting. Martha let the pastor know that Jade wanted to still be a member of New Walk. He gave her the message given to him for all members; she agreed to obey, and they continued the meeting.

Jade raised her hand and said, "What are we going to do about the scandal against the church?"

Martha said, "Cole the minister of music is planning to tear down at the time that we are trying to build up. We will not let this block our way. It seems like a whole lot is coming against us corporately and individually. We have to remember that there are a lot of us than it is of them. How bad do we want it is the question to be answered, not what are we going to do about the giant that has come against us." Pastor Gavin stood up to address the people. He thanked Martha for all her help, thanked Milo for taking the position of youth leader, and thanked the rest of the members that were in the room.

After his address, he asked if there was anything more needed to be discussed before he closed out the meeting. Milo asked if Jade could be his assistant. The minister agreed knowing that she had some experience with the youth. Mrs. Queen always talked very highly of her. Jade could not believe that Mrs. Queen had talked very favorably of her. It blew her away that the person she thought was so ruthless and cold turned out to be so kind and compassionate and loving towards her, especially what she did to him.

Pastor Gavin said, "There are some that are going around spreading rumors, but we must play that game and win. Persecution has come to stop us from doing what we have planned to do for the church. We must leave these four walls and spread the word. Are you willing to do what must be done for this church to go forth?"

Everyone spoke at the same time that they were willing. Gavin let them know that fear must not reign. They must not let the opposition kill what is inside of them. They need to take their gifts to the next level. When the opposition rises higher, they must dig deeper. They are being taught how to reach for the betterment. This is the purpose and destiny that needs to be met. He captured their attention, then gave them their marching orders. He gave them something to believe in. He activated what was inside them, pulling out their talents and gifts so they could shine. Unleashing the power and getting a chain reaction. Emotions are running high, pain, depression, grief, they have their work cut out for them.

Everyone in that room lives have been changed. Now they are required to put in the work that will bring changes in others lives. New Walk Baptist Church will turn this city upside down to find these people. They have the idea, now it is time to activate it. With the world dying, it is a necessity to spark the fire upon the darkness and let life arise. They are bringing heaven down to earth.

Martha closed the meeting out with a prayer, "Father, we are gathered here today to give thanks for what is already done. We do not battle against humans but principalities, spiritual wickedness, the rulers of the darkness. Therefore we must take up our whole armor that we may be able to stand in the days of evil. Surrounding ourselves with the truth, putting on righteousness, walking in peace, and above all take the shield of faith to quench the fiery darts of the wicked ones. Watch over us so that we can speak boldly as we ought to speak when the time comes." In unison all said amen. Martha continued saying, "Even though ungodliness had crept into this church. People doing ungodly acts, turning the grace of God into impurity corrupted themselves. Rebelled, falling in their lusts, they only served themselves. They became clouds without water carried about by the winds. Like trees without fruit, like raging waves of the sea. They will be convicted of all ungodly deeds which have been committed. From their mouths, they spoke swelling words, flattering others to gain advantage. Mockers walk according to their own lust, these are vultures who cause divisions. If New Walk Baptist Church builds themselves up in faith, continue to pray, keep themselves in love, walk with compassion, they will win." She dismissed the meeting and waited for the day to begin building.

****

Cole and the rest of the gang gathered at Mrs. Nina's place, the Christian bookstore. They are ready to pounce on their prey, they are plotting a perfect scheme.

Spreading rumors so deep, so the people will not listen to anything they say. The fall of New Walk will be their great reward. Cole has hatred in his heart against Pastor Gavin for the way he treated them. This hatred has led him to discuss murdering Martha, Gavin, and Milo. He was not going to let them rebuild the church without them present. Because of the good that is happening through Gavin, Martha, Milo, and the members of New Walk, hostility is growing step by step.

They do not dare take them by force, their only recourse is through trickery. He vowed they will not stop till they are dead. They who conspired to attack New Walk left the bookstore. Bella overheard the ambush and called Martha. She picked up the phone. Bella began to tell what was being planned by Cole when Martha asked her to hold on. She answered the house phone; pastor Gavin let her know that the youth center and church had been burned down.